The Quick Instructional Planner

Training Associates
999 West Broadway, Suite 720
Vancouver BC V5Z 1K5
Canada
Fax (604) 738-4080

Canadian Cataloguing in Publication Data
Renner, Peter
    The (Quick) Instructional Planner

ISBN 0-9690465-6-1

1. Instructional systems - Design.
2. Instructional systems - Planning.
3. Adult Education. I. Training Associates II. Title
LB1028.35.R45 1988 371.3'028 C88-091392-4

Printed in Canada
Hignell Printing, Winnipeg, MB

5   4   3

The Quick Instructional Planner

Peter Renner

A learn-as-you-go
guide that takes
you from rough
idea to well-crafted
course plan.

TRAINING
ASSOCIATES
—LTD—

Ancora imparo
Still I am learning

— Michelangelo (1475-1564)

About the author

Dr. Peter Renner has worked as a self-employed instructor/
trainer/facilitator for 30 years and now lives on a small island
off Canada's west coast. He holds degrees in counselling, adult
education, and educational leadership from Simon Fraser
University and the University of British Columbia. His
publications include the best-selling *The art of teaching adults.*
Concurrent with his personal development, his practice now
focusses on narrative research, autobiographical learning, and
contemplative living. Please visit www.peter-renner.com for
recent developments and to read/download selected chapters
from his books.

HOW TO USE THIS BOOK

*T*he **Planner** is loaded with field-tested ideas, helpful tips, planning charts, checklists, and pull-out worksheets. With a steady hand, ten essential steps take you through a process that could easily become confusing. Allowing for flexibility and local conditions, it addresses some of these key issues:

Where do I start?

What content should I include?

What is 'important' and what 'nice to know'?

How do I use the talents of content experts?

Who else can I involve in the planning process?

How do I sequence course components?

Which teaching techniques are most suitable?

What print resources are there to guide and inform me?

How do I plan for active learning situations?

How do I gauge and allot time for each component?

When and how do I allow for assessment and evaluation?

How do I keep track of the teaching aids and resources?

Chances are, you will face these and related questions at the outset and along the way. You may be looking for a helping hand or be tempted to reject the structure of this (or any other) ten-step approach. Please suspend your judgment for a little while and look through the book. Once you have a grasp of the practical nature of each element, you can begin just about anywhere—as long as you attend to all ten steps at one point. In the end, you can count on the **Planner** as your faithful and competent companion on the road to a well-thought-out course design.

HERE ARE THE 10 STEPS

one IDENTIFYING TOPICS *1*
What should be included in the course?

two SELECTING TOPICS *13*
Which components are the most/least important?

three WRITING THE TITLE *23*
How to capture the intent of the course.

four DRAFTING A COURSE DESCRIPTION *31*
What is this course all about? What can
potential learners expect for their money?

five SPECIFYING OBJECTIVES *37*
What would you like the participants to be *able
to do* or *to know* when the course is over?

six DEFINING TEACHING POINTS *51*
Which points must be covered, which skills
acquired? What is to be the *content?*

seven SELECTING TEACHING TECHNIQUES *63*
Which training techniques are most appropriate?

eight BUILDING IN EVALUATION *75*
How will you measure the learners' progress?
How will success be determined?

nine DESIGNATING RESOURCES *87*
Which materials, equipment, and facilities
will be needed?

ten REVISING YOUR PLAN *97*
Plan, test, revise — and plan again.

APPENDIX *101*
Ten tear-out and reproducible worksheets

RESOURCES

To assist you in the research and planning process, take advantage of the resources on pages 28, 29, 48, 49, 60, 61, 85, 100 and 101. These practical books and articles may be available in your public or college library, through the Internet, or from your instructor.

At first glance, this step-by-step model seems rigid. (But it will only seem that way until you have understood the process.) I suggest that the first time around you follow the Steps in a straight line, not omitting one or changing the prescribed order of things.

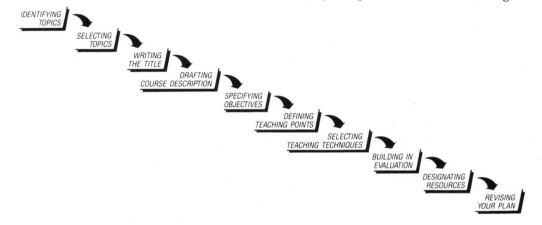

Once you understand how *QUIP* works and how it works *for you*, cut loose and move freely through the Steps. Start anywhere and skip around. You may feel like approaching planning as a circular activity, with an ongoing flow of activity and reflection. Step 1 leads to 2, to 3, and so on to Step 10. Eventually, Step 10 sets the scene for a review and a redefinition of Steps 1 and 2.

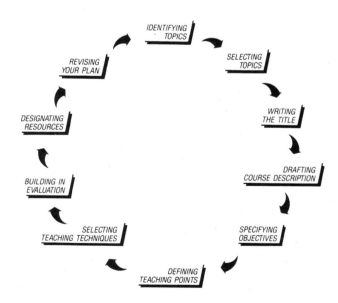

Another view of the 10 Steps is as a recurring feedback process. Here you are looking back on the previous Step for guidance, before advancing to the next. In turn, each Step has a retroactive effect on those that came before.

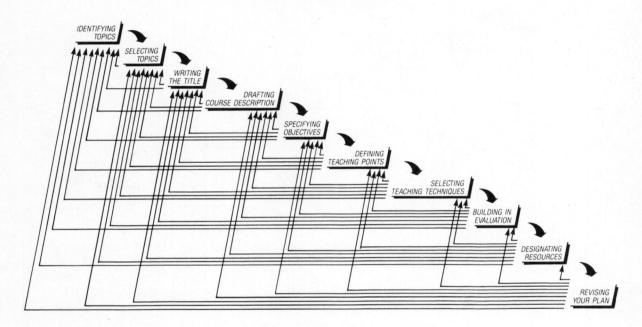

In practice, it makes little difference which way you view the Steps or how you apply them. As long as you pay attention to each of the 10 Steps, your planning will be solid.

QUIP has a wide range of applications. You can use it to:

♦ work alone, designing a course for which you are also the content specialist. Here, *QUIP* prompts you to consider the salient planning points and acts as your friend and secret consultant.

♦ assume the role of planning consultant, assisting one or more content specialists to convert their knowledge into a course design. Here, *QUIP* gives you the confidence to work with *any* topic, any expert, regardless of what you know about the subject matter.

♦ be part of a planning committee, where every member has a different agenda. Here, *QUIP* acts as the group's leader, keeping everyone on task.

The 10 Steps may not be a great revelation to you; they are just common sense and they work! *QUIP* will take you through each Step with:

♦ an introduction to set the scene and give you a rationale for the Step;

♦ some examples, drawn from my experience, to illustrate the desired result for the Step;

♦ a call for action to prompt you to apply the Step to your own work;

♦ assorted handy hints to help you take full advantage of *QUIP*;

♦ bibliographical tips to lead you beyond the basics.

DEFINITIONS

You will come across these terms throughout *QUIP*:

Learner: This is the person who will attend the course. Synonyms: student, participant, attendee.

Course: Denotes the educational event you are designing. Synonyms: presentation, workshop, seminar, symposium, session, program.

Sponsor: Refers to the person or organization that is behind this course. Synonyms: boss, client, school, company, institution, agency, organization.

Trainer: This is the person who conducts the course; it may be you or someone else. Synonyms: instructor, presenter, teacher, facilitator.

Cooperator: People you consult for various reasons during the planning process. Synonyms: expert, colleague, boss, consultant, friend, spouse, man-in-the-street.

The Quick Instructional Planner

A learn-as-you-go
guide that takes
you from rough
idea to well-crafted
course plan.

one

Every act of creation is first of all an act of destruction.

--Pablo Picasso

In his functioning as a facilitator of learning, the leader endeavors to recognize and accept his own limitations.

--Carl Rogers

IDENTIFYING TOPICS

Step 1 deals with a rough sorting out of what to include in the course. This Step is the freeing up and writing down of all-I-ever-wanted-to-include-in-this-course-if-I-were-God step.

Your aim for this Step is to produce a broad course description and I provide you with several idea-generating techniques in the next few pages. They are varied and probably familiar, but their application may be new to you. You choose the one that best helps you to get your creative juices flowing. Your cooperators may also need your help to prime their pumps. So, read through this entire chapter first and be prepared to think. The more ideas you can generate at this point, the better. It is always beneficial to have too much rather than too little to work with when designing a course.

This is a critical point of the design sequence. You must feel free to put all your cards on the table. This honesty will go a long way towards avoiding nasty surprises later. You are familiar with the scenario: everything is well underway when someone pipes up with "But I thought we were going to ....". Or, you are finally ready to send the handouts to the printer when you receive a memo informing you that "further to our conversation the course must . . ."

Whenever you see the following page format, you will find some practical hints from my school of experience. They are techniques and suggestions I have found useful in my planning. Try as many as you wish and adapt them to suit your style and environment.

Use the first two techniques to get yourself going. After that I'll give you two more you can use to involve others.

MAY I SUGGEST...

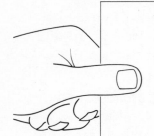

BRANCHING

Writing, by its very nature, starts at the left hand side of the page, moves to the right, then to the next line, and so on. Ideas, on the other hand, rarely come in such a neat order. My mind seems a hodge-podge of thoughts, some half-baked, some right where I need them, others off-topic. So, when I have to sort ideas into a logical order, I use a technique called *branching*. It allows me to exaggerate what is already going on in my head.

Similar to brainstorming, branching asks you to come up with as many ideas as you possibly can without judging them at the time. Branching "begins in the middle, goes back to the start, and on to the end, and then moves back to the middle again."*

You can use branching whenever you need to generate and sort ideas. Try it now to come up with possible components for your course:

1. Write the name or topic of your course in a box in the middle of a blank piece of paper. A white board or poster paper will do as well.
2. Now draw branches off that box, one for each of the main components as they occur to you. As others come to mind, either attach them to a previous branch as a sub-branch, or give them a new one by themselves. Some branches will be for *what* you want to include, others for *how* you want to achieve this.
3. Give yourself at least 10 minutes. Remember: you can always go back, add, delete or edit.
4. When you run out of ideas, step back from your picture, then add lines, arrows, connectors and extra branches, using colored pens to show relationships.

* Henriette Anne Klauser, WRITING ON BOTH SIDES OF THE BRAIN. New York: Harper & Row, 1986.

Here's a branching diagram for a course on "Effective Meetings".

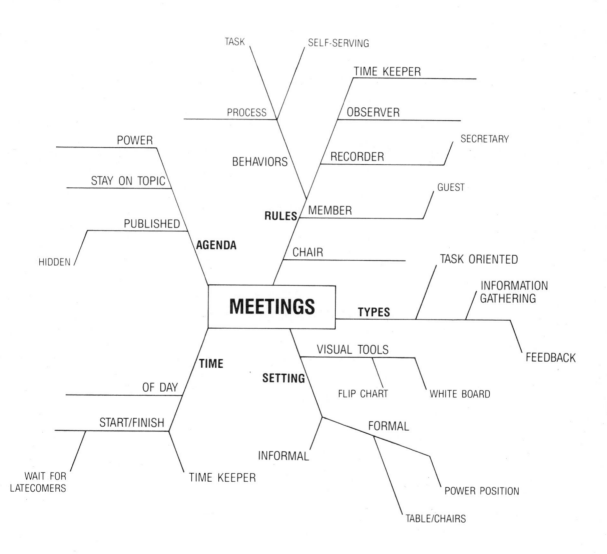

BRAINWRITING

One way to get your creative juices flowing while bypassing your built-in "critic" is to use *brainwriting**. It can help you to write down what's on (in) your mind. Follow these simple but necessary rules:

1. Set your timer for 10 minutes.
2. Have plenty of paper and your favorite pen.
3. Write the name of your course at the top of page one.
4. Now write for 10 minutes whatever comes to your mind, be it related to the content, the shape or the feel of your course.
5. Do not take your pen off the paper! If you are running dry, write about that. Your mind will soon drift back to the topic at hand.
6. When 10 minutes have gone by, but not sooner, stop writing. Shake your hand and look over what you have written.
7. With a colored marker, circle or highlight the main themes of what you have written. On a new sheet of paper, list your main themes or ideas. Add new ones as they may occur to you. If any are too slim, take a few minutes and brainwrite to expand them.

The next two techniques are ideally suited for use with several people. Decide who could be of help to you, then invite them over.

* For more on "brain patterning" and "mind mapping", read: Tony Buzan, USE BOTH SIDES OF YOUR BRAIN. New York: E.P. Dutton, 1976, and MAKE THE MOST OF YOUR MIND. New York: Linden Press-Simon & Schuster, 1984.

WISH LIST

This is one everybody knows. Ask yourself: "What if I had a magic wand, what would I like to see included in the course?" Also ask your client, your cooperators and your potential participants.

Here are the kind of responses you might come up with:

... your own wishful thinking:
"I'd like to give a course which would teach supervisors how to conduct meetings that don't bore everyone to tears *and* get the job done in the shortest time possible *and* get everyone involved *while* keeping the chairperson in charge."

. . . the manager's wishful thinking:
"I'd like you to come up with a course that would do away, once and for all, with the poor attitude some switchboard operators are displaying when dealing with guest inquiries. Give some skills training, tell them about how important their job is to our success as a hotel."

. . . past students' wishful thinking:
"We liked your course so much, but we seem to have barely scratched the surface. We want a more advanced course, where we learn some more of the background theory, some of the high-powered stuff, so that we can go out and get better jobs or be promoted."

. . . the subject specialist's wishful thinking:
"I have developed this software for small business computers. It works well and should be a bestseller. What I want to do, is develop a course around it and sell it as a package: the software together with a one-day training program. I guess you don't know much about computers, but you know teaching. Can you help me put this together?"

. . . the marketer's wishful thinking:
"We hear a lot about these straightforward, one-day seminars that are touring the country. There ought to

be a market for them in our area. I have a list of topics that would go well with hospitals and service industries. 30 to 40 people to a class, a well-organized presenter, fee below a hundred dollars, in a hotel meeting room… what do you think? Can you put something together that would fly?"

BRAINSTORMING

You have probably heard of this or used it. Essentially, the rules in brainstorming are*:

1. Write the 'problem' on a sheet of paper (or flipchart or whiteboard). It could be "What should be the components for the course?"
2. List as many ideas (components) as you can. Get help from others who either know the topic, have a say in the final design, or could be participants.
3. Do not criticize any comments. Anything goes, the crazier the better.
4. Piggy-back on the ideas of others. One idea prompts another, however similar it may appear.
5. Write every contribution down.
6. When you run dry, take a moment to read over what's been written and you may get additional ideas.
7. Stop. Possibly leave the paper hanging where others can see it. Invite them to take a pen and add their own words.
8. Only now go through the list and do some gentle editing to:
    a. eliminate duplications
    b. delete "impossible" ideas
    c. expand or contract what's left over, then
    d. sequence, rank and number them, then
    e. write them all down on fresh paper.

* For the best description of brainstorming, see: Edward de Bono, LATERAL THINKING. Penguin Books, 1977, pp. 131-146.

Here are a few examples of Step 1 planning. As you will notice, they are still in rough form, need editing and are a long way from their final wording.

From a course on "Book Publishing":

For people who have a 'book inside them' and who wish to self-publish. The course will look at all the things a first-time publisher must know: from manuscript to printed work. There will be a project that evolves from session-to-session so that by the end each person will have a working plan for their book. Must be practical.

The course will be in eight 3-hour sessions for a maximum of 20 participants. Occasional guest lecturers and a round-table discussion with other self-publishers on the last session.

From a workshop on "Conflict Resolution":

A 2-day workshop for customer service supervisors to teach them techniques to deal with conflict that occurs in their work. They should learn how to intervene when there are conflicts between subordinates, but also be able to act as 'neutral' third parties and assist two disputing people to solve their conflict.

This is not an encounter group, keep focus on a systematic approach. Each participant would get a workbook to keep notes and take home. Lots of case examples, some role playing, checklists, use video? Would be nice to have a co-instructor for the small group activities to keep them on track.

WORKSHEET

A note on the use of this and other work sheets. They are indicated here in miniature, but located in their full size in the Appendix. You may make photocopies of those marked "Reproduced with Permission" for use in planning your course. I suggest you keep them in a binder together with other materials you accumulate in the process.

Write down your ideas for the course you are planning. Keep your "critic" off to the side. It is virtually impossible to be creative *and* critical at the same time!

Let your thoughts flow freely from your brain to the paper. Do not edit! As you think of what is possible and what is not, "park" those thoughts for the time being. Concentrate instead on the kind of event you (or your client) would like to see. Imagine you have a magic wand.

Worksheet 1: *IDENTIFYING TOPICS*

Course Title:

_____

Topics to be included:

1. _____
2. _____
3. _____
4. _____
5. _____
6. _____
7. _____
8. _____
9. _____
10. _____
11. _____

MAY I SUGGEST...

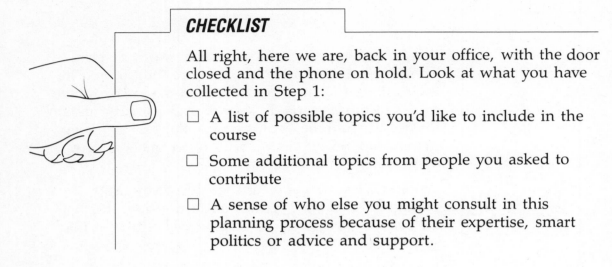

CHECKLIST

All right, here we are, back in your office, with the door closed and the phone on hold. Look at what you have collected in Step 1:

☐ A list of possible topics you'd like to include in the course

☐ Some additional topics from people you asked to contribute

☐ A sense of who else you might consult in this planning process because of their expertise, smart politics or advice and support.

NOTES

t w o

Creative thinkers make many false starts, and continually waver between unmanageable fantasies and systematic attack.

--Henry Hepner

I don't know about the key to success, but the key to failure is trying to please everyone.

--Bill Cosby

SELECTING TOPICS

*Y*our assignment for Step 2 is to sort through the mass of opinions and determine which topics are most important and must be included; which are least important and can be omitted; and which are nice to include if you can justify them.

Although your door should be closed, your mind *must* remain open. Keep your cooperators involved. Go back to them as you refine the list, seek their input, give them a sense of involvement and ownership. Have you thought of talking to potential participants and sundry subject experts? How about those who hold the purse strings, those who will decide who attends, and those who will market the course?

By the conclusion of this Step, you will have determined the territory you wish to cover with this course. Not every item generated in Step 1 will survive this sifting process. You must refine a list of topics so that you can develop your course description later.

In the end, however, you must decide which topics to include and which to leave out.

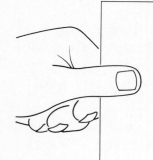

RANKING

Chances are you've ended up with more ideas than you can handle. Keep in focus what you set out to do. You won't be able to please everyone. Take the best ideas and incorporate them with what you feel, deep in your gut. Here's a suggestion to help you sort them out.

Write each potential component on a separate piece of paper.

Spread the pieces before you on a tabletop. (Alternatively, use Post-It (tm) stickers on a large sheet of paper or your office wall to make this process more visual and manageable.)

Re-shuffle your entries in two stages:

First, arrange them according to importance by placing the most important topics on the left and the least important on the right.

Second, prioritize the items in both groups. Do this (a) from the most to least important, (b) in the sequence they might be taught, or (c) according to what should come first, second and so on.

WORKSHEET

List the people who should be consulted at this stage. Think of anyone who could help refine your component list and also those whose input or blessing may be needed down the road.

(A full-size version of this work sheet is in the Appendix. Feel free to make a copy.)

Worksheet 2: *LIST OF COOPERATORS*

Name   **Why this person?**

_____   _____
_____   _____
_____   _____
_____   _____
_____   _____
_____   _____
_____   _____
_____   _____
_____   _____

Summary notes of my discussions:

_____
_____
_____
_____
_____
_____
_____
_____
_____
_____

WORKSHEET

One basic rule of marketing dictates that you must "determine the needs of the market, then create the product or service to meet that need." The course designer's focus must be equally clear. Do not go another Step in the planning process without gathering some information about who the audience will be. For whom are you designing this course? How can you describe the intended participants in terms such as: expectations, learning style, age, gender, work and school experience, reason for coming?

This information may be of a general nature to describe a group of people, but it will be vital when you make planning decisions such as the determination of content.

The worksheet lists the most obvious data to be collected. Feel free to add your own. To obtain the information, seek out your collaborators, especially those who:

♦ are expected to attend
♦ will be sent
♦ will do the sending
♦ may have taught a similar group before
♦ gave you the idea for the course.

You have the choice to ask them informally ("How would you describe the participants?") or formally ("Here is a questionnaire...") This sample is just one possibility. Design your own and ask the questions you always wanted to. Then compile a composite picture of your future students.

Worksheet 3: *PARTICIPANT PROFILE*

You can help us design a course on _____.
We want to make sure that we develop a course that meets the learning needs of people like you. Please complete this brief questionnaire with as much detail as you wish. It should take no more than 5 minutes of your time.

Your name (optional) _____

Your present job title or occupational function:

_____

_____

How many years have you held your present title or performed your occupational function: _____ years

Your gender: Female / Male

Your age group: Between 20 and 30
(check one)   between 30 and 40
                    between 40 and 50
                    between 50 and 60

Briefly list any course you have taken during the last three years that may be related to the one we are planning:

_____

_____

_____

_____

_____

Which two words best describe your favorite instructor?:

_____

Which two words best describe the instructor you like least?:

_____

When I began work on a "Conflict" course, I kept notes of the comments my cooperators gave me:

> The education chairman at the Chamber of Commerce was interested in sponsoring the event, "if you can offer it to retailers in the community. They are busy people; a 1-day course would be your best bet."
>
> The manager of the Dispute Settlement Center was reluctant to get involved in "anything less than a 3-day workshop. I suggest you build in lots of practice and role playing."
>
> Two owners of small businesses in the neighborhood told me that "this is a good idea, as long it's not longer than half a day. None of us could spare more". Both mentioned "criticism-giving and receiving" as timely topics.
>
> The manager of human resources for an airline suggested that such a course should be for "teams of two or more people from a given organization to better transfer the new information".
>
> My former counseling professor wanted to get involved, possibly as instructor. She suggested that I "add a section on power as this is often the root cause of conflict situations".
>
> After bouncing my course ideas off these people and letting their comments effect my thinking, I renamed the course "Conflict & Criticism". I also made a list of the topics to be included:

1. Myths about conflict
2. Overcoming the fear of confrontation
3. Giving negative and positive criticism
4. Receiving negative and positive criticism
5. Recognizing and controlling your anger
6. Responding to anger in others
7. Sources of power and how to use them
8. The 5-step method to working out conflict with another person
9. Transferring learning through personal action plans.

WORKSHEET

After consultation and reflection, write up your list of most important topics.

Worksheet 4: MOST IMPORTANT TOPICS

Course: _____

The most **important** topics are:

* _____

* _____

* _____

* _____

* _____

* _____

* _____

* _____

MAY I SUGGEST...

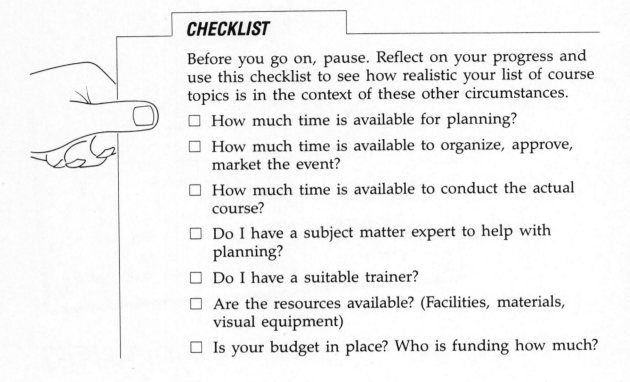

CHECKLIST

Before you go on, pause. Reflect on your progress and use this checklist to see how realistic your list of course topics is in the context of these other circumstances.

☐ How much time is available for planning?

☐ How much time is available to organize, approve, market the event?

☐ How much time is available to conduct the actual course?

☐ Do I have a subject matter expert to help with planning?

☐ Do I have a suitable trainer?

☐ Are the resources available? (Facilities, materials, visual equipment)

☐ Is your budget in place? Who is funding how much?

NOTES

three

Write for an audience of one and hope
the rest of the world will like it.

--Kurt Vonnegut

If you can't be funny,
be interesting.

--Harold Ross

WRITING THE TITLE

*T*he time has come to name the baby. You may have been using a working title until now ("The management course", or "The estimating workshop"), but a more precise and descriptive title is possible after the research in Steps 1 and 2.

The effective course title conveys two things: what it will cover (content) and how it will do so (process). In many instances, the title will be all a potential learner hears or reads. On this brief description rest many enrollment decisions. Many people, including those responsible for funding, approval or promotion, form opinions and pass judgement on the title alone. Some won't read past it. Others will be intrigued, informed and sold.

Understanding Wines

TEACHING ADULTS

Fundraising Fundamentals

Bird-watching 101

The Use of Narrative in Teaching

ACCOUNTING for DUMMIES

Oriental Brush Painting

For an example, go back to Step 1 and the course on "book publishing". That title conveys very little. It has to be re-written. Can you think of one that paints a more lively picture of the content and process?

_____

_____

_____

What do you make of these?

"How to publish your first book", or
"Publish it yourself: a hands-on workshop for enterprising authors".

Do they give you a better feel for content and process?

A second example is a course on "conflict resolution". The initial change from "Conflict Resolution" to "Conflict & Criticism" made the topic more palatable. Can you think of an even better one?

_____

_____

_____

My refinements:

"How to Manage Conflict & Criticism in the Workplace", or
"How to Handle Conflict: a Workshop for Supervisors".

WORKSHEET

Worksheet 5: *COURSE TITLE*

Complete this worksheet in 4 stages.

1. Fill in the title you have been using in your preliminary planning. Put down also the one traditionally used in your setting.

   _____

   _____

2. Re-write the old title. Try for active verbs that convey the flavor of what you envisage.

   _____

   _____

3. Check it against each criterion below. Add your own as they occur to you. Take corrective action if you are unable to place a checkmark against an item.

The course title . . .

   ☐ conveys the content.
   ☐ gives a sense of the process.
   ☐ uses clearly understood words.
   ☐ fits into the list of other courses offered.
   ☐ meets the approval of the sponsor.
   ☐ _____

4. Show just the title to your cooperators. What do they *think* the course is about? Does their interpretation match your intention? Record their impressions, then revise (if necessary) or be satisfied (if the title conveyed your message fully).

Record of reactions

   _____

   _____

   _____

   _____

   _____

   _____

   _____

   _____

   _____

   _____

MAY I SUGGEST...

LEARNER ASSESSMENT

At this point I advise you to pause again. Consider your audience.

1. Are your intended learners prepared to take your course? Do they possess the prerequisite information and skills to fully participate in and benefit from your course?
2. Do any (or all) of your intended learners already have some or all of the skills and information you plan to include in the final program?

If you are unsure of the answers, your course is in danger of failing. You may plan a very good course, select the best material possible and hire a trainer with the finest credentials, but the final delivery could still be a flop, because someone forgot to check if the audience was ready for it.

How can you find out how ready your students are, or is the design such that it requires no special prerequisite? Select from these to suit your situation:

♦ clearly spell out prerequisites in the course description so that applicants can decide their entry qualifications:

   Applicants must...
   . . . have first-year university algebra
   . . . have directly supervised at least five clerks
   . . . be familiar with Lotus 1-2-3
   . . . possess a first-aid ticket, Level III
   . . . be newcomers to the industry.

◆ divide the course into two sections, with a stipulation that Part I has to be completed successfully before Part II may be entered.

In this situation you must decide how to deal with people who claim to have the Part I experience. Can you insist that they all take both parts or is there a way to test applicants? Is there a standard certificate or licence that could serve as evidence of their ability?

◆ provide an assessment procedure which any applicant must undergo.

Based on the results, you can design a course that suits the measured ability of your audience. You would no longer be guessing but have measurable evidence of your learners' skills and knowledge.

Theory, models, overviews

Brady, M. (1989). *What's worth teaching? Selecting, organizing, and integrating knowledge.* Albany, NY: State University of New York Press.

Cunningham, P. M. (1993). Let's get real: a critical look at the practice of adult education. *Journal of Adult Education, 22,* 1, 3-15. Available: www.nl.edu/ace/Resources/Documents/Cunningham.html

Elias, J. L., & Merriam, S. B. (1995). *Philosophical foundations of adult education.* Malabar, FL: Krieger.

Houle, C. O. (1992). *The literature of adult education: a bibliographic essay.* San Francisco: Jossey-Bass.

Kolb, D. A. (1984). *Experiential learning.* Englewood Cliffs, NJ: Prentice Hall.

Merriam, S. B., & Brockett, R. G. (1996). *The profession and practice of adult education: an introduction.* San Francisco: Jossey-Bass.

Pratt, D. D. (1998). *Five perspectives on teaching in adult and higher education.* Malabar, FL: Krieger Publishing Co.

Talmadge, C. G. (Ed.). (1999). *Providing culturally relevant adult education: a challenge for the twenty-first century.* San Francisco: Jossey-Bass.

Wilson, A. L., & Hayes, E. R. (Eds.). (2000). *Handbook of adult and continuing education.* San Francisco: Jossey-Bass.

Publishers' web sites

Allyn & Bacon	www.vig.abacon.com/
HRD Press	www.hrdpress.co
Jossey-Bass	www.josseybass.com
Krieger	www.krieger-publishing.com
Pfeiffer/Jossey-Bass	www.pfeiffer.com
Teachers College Press	www.teacherscollegepress.com/
Training Associates	www.peter-renner.com/books.htm
Yahoo book search	www.shopping.yahoo.com/books/

Adult learning

Belenky, M. F., & others (1997). *Women's ways of knowing*. New York: Basic Books.

Boud, D., & Griffin, V. (Eds.). (1985). *Appreciating adults learning: from the learners' perspective*. London: Kogan Page.

Brookfield, S. D. (1986). *Understanding and facilitating adult learning*. San Francisco: Jossey Bass.

Cranton, P. (1994). *Understanding and promoting transformative learning: a guide for educators of adults*. San Francisco: Jossey-Bass.

Cranton, P. (1997). *Transformative learning in action: insights from practice*. New Directions of Adult and Continuing Education, No. 74. San Francisco: Jossey-Bass.

Galbraith, M. W. (Ed.). (1990). *Adult learning methods: a guide for effective instruction*. Malabar, FL: Krieger.

Hayes, E., Flannery, D. D., & Associates (2000). *Women as learners: the significance of gender in adult learning*. San Francisco: Jossey-Bass.

Knowles, M. S. (1992). *The adult learner: a neglected species*. (2nd ed.). Houston, TX: Gulf Publishing

Long, H. B. (2001). *Teaching for learning*. Malabar, FL: Krieger Publishing.

Merriam, S. B., & Caffarella, R. S. (1999). *Learning in adulthood: a comprehensive guide*. (2nd ed.). San Francisco: Jossey-Bass.

Mezirow, J., & Associates (2000). *Learning as transformation: critical perspectives on a theory in progress*. San Francisco: Jossey-Bass.

Piskurich, G. M. (1993). *Self-directed learning: a practical guide to design, development, and implementation*. San Francisco: Jossey-Bass.

Tennant, M. & Pogson, P. (1995). *Learning and change in the adult years: a developmental perspective*. San Francisco: Jossey-Bass.

four

*If you're not sure where you're going,
you're liable to end up someplace else.*

--Robert Mager

DRAFTING A COURSE DESCRIPTION.

While your new title is designed to catch the reader's fancy, your course description follows through with details on what will be in the course and how it will be accomplished.

The course description serves the needs of key players in the planning process:

The **planner** becomes clear on *what* this course will cover and *how* it will occur. The description becomes the initial anchor point for the remaining planning Steps. When things get confusing later, you can always look back to see, "What *was* the intent of this course? What did I set out to create?"

The **trainer** is informed of the content to teach and the atmosphere to create in the classroom. Unless the planner also becomes the instructor, the course still has to be handed over to someone to teach it. A course description serves as the initial selection tool. "Can you teach this material?", "Is she qualified to teach at this level?", "Will he be comfortable to run such a participatory course?"

The **learner** finds out what she/he can expect to learn in the course and what kind of participation is expected. The course description must be clear on prerequisites, course outcome and method of instruction.

The **sponsor** can determine the suitability of the course. Does this course fit into the lineup of others? Is it what we want to offer?

EXAMPLES

Here are a few sample paragraphs taken from published course announcements. As you will find, different writers take different tacks. See which appeals to you so that you can follow that example when you write your course description.

From "Writing Briefs: Making Your Case to Government" (Simon Fraser University, Vancouver, BC):

"Governments are so inundated with information it's hard to get their attention. What will help to make them take notice is a coherent, well-developed brief that states the presenter's case clearly and forcefully. This two-day course is designed to help individuals and organizations make a successful case to government."

From "Understanding Wines: a course for restaurant employees" (British Columbia Institute of Technology, Vancouver, BC):

"In this 9-session, introductory course you can learn how to identify, select, taste, store, and serve still and sparkling wines. Topics include: influence of growing conditions, grape varieties, wine-making, marketing, labelling laws, quality classifications. Emphasis will be on the presentation and selling of wines in restaurants. Each session will consist of a lecture presentation with films and slides, guided discussions, written quizzes and a sensory evaluation of six wines."

From "Financial Analysis and Planning Using Lotus 1-2-3" (Control Data Institute for Advanced Technology, St. Paul, MN):

"This is an intensive three-day seminar presenting an array of useful financial analysis techniques, combined with the ease and power of Lotus 1-2-3. The emphasis is on how to apply this powerful spreadsheet to business finance solutions. Attenders will learn how to develop ready-to-use programs that can later be modified to suit their companies' needs. Case studies will be used to simulate real-world problems."

From "Successful Direct Marketing" (SDM Schrello Direct Marketing, Long Beach, CA):

"Please don't confuse this program with any other. This course is designed and conducted *by* and *for* those in the training, information and education business. In two exciting, fast-moving days, "Successful Direct Marketing" covers every critical phase of selecting, adapting and promoting information and training products and services. Each session is packed with specific, easy-to-understand and easy-to-use "insider" tips and how-to-do-it techniques distilled by Don Schrello from his personal experience ..."

Worksheet 6: *COURSE DESCRIPTION*

1. Write your description. Start off where your course title ends, enlarge upon it and anticipate the reader's questions.

---

2. Read the questions that follow and honestly evaluate your work.

   My course description . . .

   ☐ conveys the course content.
   ☐ gives a sense of the process.
   ☐ uses clearly understood words.
   ☐ indicates level of instruction and prerequisites.
   ☐ informs potential trainers.
   ☐ informs potential participants.
   ☐ meets the approval of the sponsor.
   ☐ fits the brochure / calendar in style and length.
   ☐ says exactly what I want it to say.
   ☐ _____

3. If you think that your description "fails" any of these, re-write until it "passes". Then be satisfied!

4. Show your shiny new title and course description to at least one cooperator. See your Worksheet #2 for the names of the people you consulted earlier. Record their reaction. Incorporate their ideas.

NOTES

five

Many identify training with the process [of teaching] dogs to sit, roll over, and retrieve.

--Irwin J. Jahns

SPECIFYING OBJECTIVES

*C*ongratulations! You are now ready to begin Step 5 of the planning process. The good news is that, once you have completed it, you'll be half-way through.

You are entering the Step where you specify objectives. I'm sure that sounds ominous. Even the most seasoned course developers and trainers squirm at the mention of "'it's time to write objectives". The mere hint of the word *objectives* sends many into a frenzy of bathroom visits, coffee breaks, memo reading, pencil sharpening, or some other such "creative procrastination". I ask you to now engage in your favorite avoidance behavior for a maximum of 10 minutes and when you return, join *QUIP* in exploring ... objectives.

Welcome back. I assure you that the work you put into this Step will pay off for you. Once you've written down objectives, you will feel a sense of relief and direction. No longer will you feel fuzzy about what you wish to accomplish with this course.
For a comparison, think of vacation planning. Every year some of us talk of going on a vacation, but it is only after we have picked a specific destination that we feel that we are going places. Stating a destination allows us to click into action: sending for brochures, booking flights, phoning friends, checking our wardrobe, starting another diet, and so on. Similarly, once you have written your course objectives, you can actively start planning the surrounding details for your training event.

Objectives are formal expressions of the desired outcome of a course. There are three types:

1. Planning objectives
2. Process objectives
3. Learning objectives

Let's begin with the least complicated type; a *planning objective* describes the "must do's" with which you have to work. Examples:

- ◆ the course *must* be ready in time for the managers' retreat.
- ◆ it *must* be no longer than 2 days.
- ◆ the new video library *must* be utilized (to justify recent equipment purchases)
- ◆ the course *must* be delivered by our own training staff
- ◆ this course *must* serve as prototype for future in-house events.

So, get started on the planning objectives for your course (Worksheet 7). Make full use of the information you gathered in the previous four Steps, especially the expectations expressed by your cooperators.

WORKSHEET

Worksheet 7: PLANNING OBJECTIVES

Course Title: _____

My planning objectives are:

* _____
_____

* _____
_____

* _____
_____

* _____
_____

* _____

With the planning objectives underway, take a sneak preview of the second member of the objectives family.

Process objectives are hard to define. They are the objectives which everybody talks about, but has such a difficult time specifying. A few examples will illustrate that point:

> The participants should come away from the event with:

♦ an *increased confidence* in their role as leaders of people
♦ a *better commitment* to teamwork
♦ an *expanded willingness* to critique their own meeting style
♦ a *renewed* sense of *accomplishment*
♦ a *new appreciation* for the expenditure of training time and money.

In effect, process objectives reflect your own and others' Christmas wish list. They allow you to express ("Wouldn't it be nice, if ...") the attitudinal learning outcomes of training. Although they are expressed in "soft" terms, their definition early in the game is absolutely vital. They are the beacons in the night, guiding planner, trainer and learner toward a successful course.

Now write the process objectives for your course (Worksheet 8). Utilize all the information you have gathered to this point. Especially note the off-hand comments and between-the-lines messages your cooperators have sent.

WORKSHEET

Worksheet 8: PROCESS OBJECTIVES

Course Title: _____

My process objectives are:

*   _____
    _____

*   _____
    _____

*   _____
    _____

*   _____
    _____

*   _____
    _____

*   _____
    _____

*   _____
    _____

*   _____
    _____

*   _____
    _____

*   _____
    _____

You are moving along very nicely! So, what's the big deal with these objectives, you might ask. Wait, here they come (drumroll, please), the greatest planning obstacle known to trainers: *learning objectives*! Their purpose is to spell out what the learner should be able to do, know, or feel as the result of successful instruction.

Some instructional designers and theoreticians are adamant that these be spelled out in great detail early in the planning process. In my experience, most trainers find it very difficult to envisage such details in advance. The broad course outline may be clear, a list of topics may be apparent, but to generate a complete list of learning objectives is hard. My solution to the dilemma is to gradually develop a pool of objectives, to be refined, enlarged, edited, and finally accepted as the course plan evolves.

Learning objectives state the *outcome* of instruction in terms of what behavior the learner *will be able to do*. In the final analysis, it is the learner who must do the learning. The instructor is responsible for the setting and the information. The learner is responsible for the acquisition of the skills, the digestion of the information and the development of his or her attitudes and emotions. Learning objectives allow us to specify and measure the learning that takes place. Objectives state in straight language, "For this course to be a success, this is what the learner must be able to do or must know at the conclusion of instruction."

These examples are from a course on "how to be a travel counselor".

Topic: How to read a map.

Learning objectives:
Given a map, the students *will be able to* . . . .

a. *explain* the use of a map scale.
b. *calculate* the distance between two towns.
c. *identify* the map symbols and explain an example of each.

From a course on "managing meetings".

Topic: Problem-solving meetings

Learning objectives:
The learner *will be able to* . . .

a. *distinguish* between an informational and a problem-solving meeting.
b. *define* the difference between process and content interventions.
c. *list* ten common meeting problems and suggest remedies.
d. *demonstrate*, in practice meetings, how to keep a group on topic.

MAY I SUGGEST...

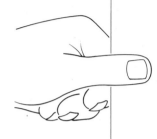

WRITING CLEAR OBJECTIVES

A sure way to get your creative juices flowing in the task of writing learning objectives, is to start each with an *action verb*. Here's a list of such verbs, each with an example to get you going.

If your topic deals with the development of artistic behavior, incorporate these action verbs:
- ◆ paint
- ◆ build
- ◆ design
- ◆ construct
- ◆ draw
- ◆ illustrate.

Example:
Given the space requirements, the learner will be able to *design* a basic greenhouse.

If your topic has to do with language behavior:
- ◆ abbreviate
- ◆ edit
- ◆ spell
- ◆ pronounce
- ◆ paraphrase
- ◆ translate.

Example:
Given a short paragraph, the learner will be able to edit it, using the three 'cutting deadwood' rules provided in the textbook.

For mathematical skills:
- add
- calculate
- prove
- divide
- measure
- verify.

Example:
Given daily operating statistics, the learner will be able to calculate the average room rate per occupied hotel room.

For social behaviors:
- discuss
- elaborate
- contribute
- demonstrate.

Example: While leading a small group in a problem-solving task, the participant will be able to demonstrate the three basic facilitation skills explained in the film.

If you need more help on objective writing, turn to the following old chestnuts. Any library worth its turnstiles should have at least one of them. Robert Mager's makes a humorous and convincing case for clear objectives in adult education.

Robert Mager, PREPARING INSTRUCTIONAL OBJECTIVES (2nd ed.). Belmont, CA: D.S. Lake Publ., 1984

Norman Gronlund, STATING BEHAVIORAL OBJECTIVES FOR CLASSROOM INSTRUCTION (3rd ed.). New York: The Macmillan Company, 1985.

BENEFITS OF CLEAR OBJECTIVES

Learning objectives do different things for different people.

The *learner* gets a clear picture of what is expected, both during instruction and in anticipation of tests and real-life applications.

The *trainer* sees what has to be taught.

The *sponsor* likes them to decide on such things as funding approval, endorsement, staff release, accreditation.

For the *course planners*, learning objectives offer some immediate and practical benefits. With a clear picture of the end product, you can systematically plan backwards:

1. You can verify the objectives and ensure that the correct information is included in the course by consulting content specialists.
2. You can select instructional techniques that are most suited to each objective. For one objective a lecture is appropriate, for another a lecture followed by a demonstration, while yet another objective is best approached through a role play and a guided discussion. (You'll be doing this in Step 7)
3. You can design evaluation procedures. If the objective states that the learner should be able to "List the 3 emergency procedures...", or "Demonstrate the use of a breathing apparatus...", then the evaluation procedures for each are apparent. (Step 8)
4. You can specify the materials, equipment, and facilities. Some will need a set of handouts, others require the use of a video recorder. (Step 9)

Now work on your learning objectives.

You are not expected to come up with a complete list of learning objectives at this point. Inevitably, you will add some as the planning process evolves; others will need re-writing or deleting. Your assignment, for the time being, is to generate as many as you can.

The easiest way to ease into this is by looking back to Step 2 and retrieving all the topics your course must cover. Copy Worksheet 9, one for each topic. Under each topic heading, write the objectives. The sample objectives you've read on the previous pages all start off with the stem "The learner will be able to..." I suggest you, too, begin yours that way, just to get into the swing of it. After that (when it gets just a bit boring), you can easily vary the opening phrase to "The (participant, student, trainee, manager, intern, attendee) will be (expected to, required to, capable of) ..."

Over to you. I'll talk to you again in Step 6.

WORKSHEET

Worksheet 9: *LEARNING OBJECTIVES*

Topic: _____

Course Title: _____

Objectives:

1. _____
   _____
   _____
   _____

2. _____
   _____
   _____
   _____

3. _____
   _____
   _____
   _____

4. _____
   _____
   _____
   _____

5. _____
   _____
   _____
   _____

A rule of thumb: If you have to write more than five objectives per topic, you are biting off more than is practical. Split the topic into two. The grouping of objectives becomes more manageable.

RESOURCES

Planning lessons, courses, and programs

Billington, D. D. (1996). Seven characteristics of highly effective adult learning programs. Available: www.newhorizon.org/article_billington1.html

Caffarella, R. S. (1994). *Planning programs for adult learners: a practical guide for educators, trainers, and staff developers.* San Francisco: Jossey-Bass.

Cervero, R. M., & Wilson, A. L. (1994). *Planning responsibly for adult education: a guide to negotiating power and interests.* San Francisco: Jossey-Bass.

Dean, G. J. (1994). *Designing instruction for adult learners.* Malabar, FL: Krieger Publishing.

Diamond, R. M. (1997). *Designing & assessing courses and curricula.* San Francisco: Jossey-Bass.

Dirkx, J. M., & Prenger, S. M. (1997). *Planning and implementing instruction for adults: a theme-based approach.* San Francisco: Jossey-Bass.

Goody, A. E., & Kozoll, C. E. (1995). *Program development in continuing education.* Malabar, FL: Krieger Publishing.

Lee, W. W., & Owens, D. L. *Multimedia-based instructional design.* San Francisco: Jossey-Bass/Pfeiffer.

The on-line classroom

Beer, V. (2000). *Web learning fieldbook: using the world wide web to build workplace learning environments.* San Francisco: Jossey-Bass/Pfeiffer.

Cahoon, B. (Ed.). (1998). *Adult learning and the internet.* San Francisco: Jossey-Bass.

Carlliner, S., & Gery, G. (1999). *An overview of on-line learning.* Amherst, MA: HRD Press.

Driscoll, M. (1998). *Web-based training: using technology to design adult learning experiences.* San Francisco: Jossey-Bass.

Kruse, K., & Keil, J. (1999). *Technology-based training: the art and science of design, development, and delivery.* San Francisco: Jossey-Bass.

Palloff, R. M., & Pratt, K. (1999). *Building learning communities in cyberspace: effective strategies for the online classroom.* San Francisco: Jossey-Bass.

Palloff, R. M., & Pratt, K. (2001). *Lessons from the cyberspace classroom: the realities of online teaching.* San Francisco: Jossey-Bass.

Training Magazine (1998). *Online learning. Special report*. A supplement to *Training Magazine, 35*, 8, OL1-Ol22.

Weiss, R. E., Knowlton, D. S., & Speck, B. W. (Eds.). (2000). *Principles of effective teaching in the online classroom*. New Directions in Teaching and Learning, No. 84. San Francisco: Jossey-Bass.

Learners with special needs

Beatty, P. T., & Wolf, M. A. (1996). *Connecting with older adults: educational responses and approaches*. Malabar, FL: Krieger Publishing.

Gadbow, N. F., & Du Bois, D. A. (1998). *Adult learners with special needs: strategies and resources for postsecondary education and workplace learning*. Malabar, FL: Krieger Publishing.

Jordan, D. R. (1996). *Teaching adults with learning disabilities*. Malabar, FL: Krieger Publishing.

Spiritual aspects

English, L. M., & Gillen, M. A. (Eds.). (2000). *Addressing the spiritual dimensions of adult learning: what educators can do*. San Francisco: Jossey-Bass.

English, L. M., Fenwick, T., & Parsons, J. (2001). *Spirituality in adult education and training*. Malabar, FL: Krieger Publishing.

Miller, J. P. (1999). *Education and the soul: toward a spiritual curriculum*. Albany, NY: SUNY Press.

Moore, T. (Ed.). (1996). *The education of the heart*. New York: HarperCollins.

O'Reilly, M. R. (1989). *Teaching as a contemplative practice*. Portsmouth, NH: Heinemann.

Palmer, P. J. (1998). *The courage to teach: exploring the inner landscape of a teacher's life*. San Francisco: Jossey-Bass.

Weibust, P. S., & Eugene, T. L. (1994). Learning and spirituality in adulthood. In J. D. Sinncott (Ed.), *Interdisciplinary handbook of adult lifespan learning*. London: Kogan-Page.

s i x

Personally I'm always ready to learn, although I don't always like being taught.

--Winston Churchill

Learning which involves the whole person of the learner, feelings as well as intellect, is the most lasting and pervasive.

--Carl Rogers

DEFINING TEACHING POINTS

Good News! You have passed the half-way mark of your planning project and, in writing the objectives, you have completed the most difficult Step. You have worked hard and the rewards will be plentiful. (Sounds a bit like a message in a fortune cookie, doesn't it?)

Now that you know with some precision where the learners must go, you can determine *what* they need to get there. In this Step you develop the *teaching points* for each objective. Teaching points are the content of instruction; they describe the material which the trainer has to present to the learner.

Your planner role begins to expand with this Step. From now on, you wear at least two hats, that of planner and that of trainer. Whether you plan to be the trainer of this course, or hand it to another person for delivery, you must *think teaching*. Whatever you do from here on, keep your mind's eye clearly focused on the eventual interaction between instructor, learner and content.

Different teaching points appeal to different aspects of our ability to learn. They challenge us in three ways. We must either:

♦ recall, recognize or expand our *knowledge*

♦ develop our *attitudes, feeling, values* and *appreciations,* or

♦ acquire *skills* (involving tools, procedures, and techniques).

Each of these types of learning also makes a different demand on the course planner, who has to match it with a teaching strategy that best helps the learner to learn (Step 7). The next example, "making tea", illustrates how even a simple teaching situation confronts the learner with a blend of knowledge, attitude, and skill learning. (It might even prompt you to have a favorite-beverage-break).

TOPIC: Making tea.

LEARNING OBJECTIVE:

Given the appropriate equipment and materials, the learner will be able to prepare a correctly brewed pot of tea.

TEACHING POINTS:

KNOWLEDGE:

◆ different varieties of tea blends produce difference flavours: e.g. Earl Grey, Darjeeling, Irish Breakfast, English Breakfast, Prince of Wales.
◆ three factors influence taste and quality of final products:
  1. water temperature
  2. ratio of tea leaves to water
  3. brewing time.

ATTITUDE:

◆ "a watched pot never boils".
◆ proper teas is well worth the wait.
◆ there is only <u>one</u> way to make good tea.

SKILL:

◆ how to warm the pot prior to brewing
◆ correct placement of tea bag or tea ball.
◆ how to boil water and pour over leaves.
◆ how to maintain proper temperature of brewed tea.

Do you see how learning falls into the three categories? You can test yourself with the following teaching points. Assign a letter to each to indicate the type of learning:

   K = knowledge, **A** = attitude, **S** = skill.

Topic:
Wine service in a restaurant.

Learning objective:
The trainee will be able to serve a bottle of red wine to a group of guests seated at a table.

Teaching points:

1. Locate the bottle in a bin.
2. Determine correct label, especially vintage.
3. Check appearance of bottle.
4. Carry to table; avoid disturbing sediments.
5. Attract attention of host.
6. Present sealed bottle to the host.
7. Answer any questions pertaining to wine.
8. Cut capsule.
9. Draw cork with corkscrew.
10. Avoid injuries (knife, glass, capsule)
11. Present cork to host.
12. Be alert to comments/questions from guests.
13. Work swiftly, but do not appear rushed.
14. Wipe rim of bottle with clean napkin.
    . . . and so on.

(Check your answers against mine on page 56.)

MAY I SUGGEST...

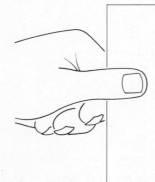

SPLITTING OBJECTIVES

As you generate teaching points for each objective, you may find that some lists get uncomfortably long. It's hard to say how long is too long, but my rule of thumb dictates: *not more than six teaching points per objective*. You'll soon develop a sense that "this objective is trying to accomplish too much". If you get to the sixth and need to add more, I suggest you either reduce the list or split the objective into two. Let me explain with an example:

EXAMPLES

Topic: **Communication skills**

Learning objective:
The student will be able to apply the paraphrasing technique in a simulated interview.

I began by asking an experienced interviewer to explain the steps she would take to reach this objective. Knowing that the course was aimed at recent recruits new to interviewing, it quickly became obvious that these people would benefit from a discussion of the theory *prior to* the practical application.

We decided to split the objective into two, generating for each some teaching points. They are in the following example, with the type of learning indicated by the letters **K**, **A** and **S**:

First learning objective:

. . . to be able to *describe* paraphrasing and give two examples from a selection interview context.

Teaching points:

K Define the term paraphrasing.
K Contrast it with other types of responses.
K Give several examples.
A Paraphrasing shows nonjudgmental listening.
A Sloppy paraphrasing creates barriers.

Second learning objective:

. . . to be able to *apply* paraphrasing in a simulated selection interview.

Teaching points:

A Make eye contact; express sincere interest. (Paraphrasing is more than a technique!)
A Avoid sounding like a parrot.
A Suspend judgement while listening.
S Pose a question, then paraphrase the answer.

ORGANIZING TEACHING POINTS

Some order to your teaching points will evolve naturally; you may have to impose more as your lists near completion. Use the criteria below to arrange and re-arrange your points until they flow. Your work in the next Steps will be much easier as a result.

Move them around, so that the teaching points for each objective build from...

♦ known facts to new facts

♦ simple concepts to complex ones

♦ the start of a process to its logical end

♦ the concrete to the abstract

♦ the safe to the risky

♦ the theoretical to the applied

(or the other way around)

Key to wine service test:

If two types of learning are involved, they are given in order of importance:

1=K	2=K	3=K
4=S,A	5=S,A	6=S
7=K,A	8=S	9=S
10=A,S	11=S	12=A,K
13=A,S	14=S	

OVER TO YOU...

Now work on your teaching points.
You need:

♦ The pull-out planning chart in the Appendix. Make several photocopies on ledger-size paper (8 1/2" x 14"), one chart for *each* objective.

♦ About 3 packages of Post-It (tm) stickers, the small ones (1/2" x 2").

Proceed as follows:

☐ Post the charts next to each other on a blank wall or punch three holes on the short side, and fold each chart so that it fits a three-ring binder.

☐ Write the first objective on a sticker and post it on the first chart, upper lefthand corner, under the heading "Objective".

☐ Write each teaching point on a sticker and place it under the heading "Teaching Points". There is room for six points. If you have more than that, see: "Splitting Objectives".

☐ If you gets stuck and can't think of the right teaching point, place a "?"-sticker and move on. The point will either come to you later or you can ask one of your cooperators for help.

☐ Record your teaching points in the order they come to you. Then go back and rearrange them. See: "Organizing Teaching Points".

☐ Label each teaching point as to type of learning: K = knowledge, A = attitude, S = skill. This information will be of great value to you when you select teaching techniques in Step 7.

☐ Take full advantage of the chart's flexibility. Move stickers around. Use different colors, (stickers or writing pen). "Park" stickers that don't seem to fit until you find their right place. Move them around to test your "what if.." inspirations.

☐ Display your charts-in-progress. Let others wander by. Enjoy the attention they'll attract. It is highly unlikely that anyone has ever seen anything like them. Finally, people will get a glimpse at the hard work you put in to plan a course. If you invite them, these onlookers may also make comments and suggestions. Listen carefully. Make a point of inviting your earlier cooperators to come and see.

☐ Stand in front of your charts and daydream. Some odd-fitting pieces will fall into place almost by themselves if you leave them alone for a while. Take the charts with you and stare at them during idle moments at the dentist's or while on the bus.

EXAMPLE

This is a partially completed planning chart.

COURSE: "THE COMPLETE BUTLER"

COMMENTS: DO THIS EARLY IN THE DAY

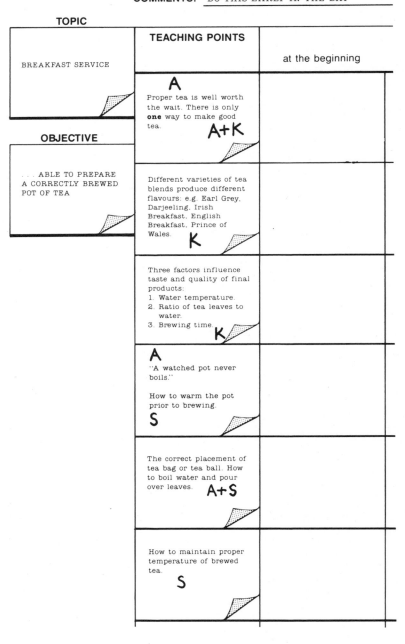

TOPIC	TEACHING POINTS	
		at the beginning
BREAKFAST SERVICE	**A** Proper tea is well worth the wait. There is only **one** way to make good tea. **A+K**	
OBJECTIVE		
... ABLE TO PREPARE A CORRECTLY BREWED POT OF TEA	Different varieties of tea blends produce different flavours: e.g. Earl Grey, Darjeeling, Irish Breakfast, English Breakfast, Prince of Wales. **K**	
	Three factors influence taste and quality of final products: 1. Water temperature. 2. Ratio of tea leaves to water. 3. Brewing time. **K**	
	A "A watched pot never boils." How to warm the pot prior to brewing. **S**	
	The correct placement of tea bag or tea ball. How to boil water and pour over leaves. **A+S**	
	How to maintain proper temperature of brewed tea. **S**	

Teaching & facilitating

Apps, J. W. (1996). *Teaching from the heart.* Malabar, FL: Krieger Publishing.

Baxter Magolda, M. B. (Ed.). (2000). *Teaching to promote intellectual and personal maturity: incorporating students' worldviews and identities into the learning process.* New Directions for Teaching and Learning, No. 82. San Francisco: Jossey-Bass.

Bess, J. L., & Associates (2000). *Teaching alone, teaching together: transforming the structure of teams for teaching.* San Francisco: Jossey-Bass.

Bligh, D. A. (2000). *What's the use of lectures?* San Francisco: Jossey-Bass.

Brockett, R. G., & Hiemstra, R. (2001). *Facilitating ethical practice in the education and training of adults: a guide for action.* Malabar, FL: Krieger Publishing.

Brookfield, S. D. (1987). *Developing critical thinkers: challenging adults to explore alternative ways of thinking and acting.* San Francisco: Jossey-Bass.

Brookfield, S. D. (1990). *The skillful teacher: on technique, trust, and responsiveness in the classroom.* San Francisco: Jossey-Bass.

Margolis, F. H., & Swan, B. J. (1999). *Trainer's handbook for participative learning.* Amherst, MA: HRD Press.

McKeachie, W. J. (1994). *Teaching tips: strategies, research, and theory for college and university teachers* (9th ed.). Lexington, MA: D.C. Heath and Co.

Pike, B. (1994). *Creative training tools: 101 ideas for increasing trainee participation.* Amherst, MA: HRD Press.

Renner, P. (1994). *The art of teaching adults: how to become an exceptional teacher and facilitator.* Vancouver, BC: Training Associates.

Silberman, M. (1990/1998). *Active training: a handbook of techniques, designs, case examples, and tips.* San Francisco: Jossey-Bass.

Silberman, M. (1995). *101 ways to make training active.* San Francisco: Jossey-Bass.

Silverman, S. L., & Casazza, M. E. (1999). *Learning and development: making connections to enhance teaching.* San Francisco: Jossey-Bass.

Sugar, S. (1998). *Games that teach: experiential activities for reinforcing learning.* San Francisco: Jossey-Bass.

Vella, J. (2000). *Taking learning to task: creative strategies for teaching adults.* San Francisco: Jossey-Bass.

Wlodkowski, R. J. (1999). *Enhancing adult motivation to learn: a comprehensive guide to teaching all adults.* San Francisco: Jossey-Bass.

RESOURCES

Coaching & mentoring

Dotlich, D. L., & Cairo, P. C. (1999). *Action coaching: how to leverage individual performance for company success.* San Francisco: Jossey-Bass.

Hudson, F. M. (1999). *The handbook of coaching: a comprehensive resource guide for managers, executives, consultants, and human resource professionals.* San Francisco: Jossey-Bass.

Bova, B., & Kroth, M. (1999). Closing the gap: the mentoring of Generation X. *Journal of Adult Education, 27*, 1, 7-17.

Cohen, N. H. (1995). *Mentoring adult learners: a guide for educators and trainers.* Malabar, FL: Krieger Publishing.

Daloz, L. A. (1999). *Mentor: guiding the journey of adult learners.* San Francisco: Jossey-Bass.

Reinarz, A. G., & White, E. R. (Eds.). (2001). *Beyond teaching and mentoring.* New Directions for Teaching and Learning, No. 85. San Francisco: Jossey-Bass.

Zachary, L. J. (2000). *The mentor's guide: facilitating effective learning strategies.* San Francisco: Jossey-Bass.

Audiovisual

Pike, B. (1994). *Powerful audiovisual techniques: 101 ideas to increase the impact of your training.* Amherst, MA: HRD Press.

Group processes & techniques

Brookfield, S. D., & Preskill, S. (1999). *Discussion as a way of teaching: tools and techniques for democratic classrooms.* San Francisco: Jossey-Bass.

Johnson, D. W., & Johnson, F. P. (2000). *Joining together: group theory and group skills.* (7th ed.). Boston, MA: Allyn & Bacon.

Quinlivan-Hall, D., & Renner, P. (1994). *In search of solutions: 60 ways to lead your problem-solving groups.* Vancouver, BC: Training Associates.

Schwarz, R. M. (1994). *The skilled facilitator: practical wisdom for developing effective groups.* San Francisco: Jossey-Bass.

Wilson, G. L. (1996). *Groups in context: leadership and participation in small groups.* (4th ed.). New York: McGraw-Hill.

seven

The evil of men is that they want to be teachers of others.

--Mencius

It is in fact nothing short of a miracle that the modern methods of instruction have not yet entirely strangled the holy curiosity of inquiry.

--Albert Einstein

SELECTING TEACHING TECHNIQUES

I won't start off by saying that you are almost there and that you can be proud of the work you have done. (But *you* may say that to yourself or even tell someone who cares.)

In this Step you'll continue to build on the foundation laid in Step 5 in which you specified *where* your learners are going to go (objectives) and in Step 6, where you decided on *what* they will have to learn to get there (teaching points). In this Step you are concerned with *how* the trainer will facilitate that learning.

You must pick teaching techniques that will set the tone and tempo for the course. Your choice will define the quality of interaction between trainer, learner and course content. Teaching techniques include: lectures, guided discussion, small group projects, role playing, viewing of films, field trips, debate and case discussion.

The chosen techniques, each matched to a teaching point, will serve as "stage directions" for the person who will deliver the course. Often the designer and the trainer are separate persons. If that is the case, your directions must be able to "stand alone" to enable someone other than yourself to bring them to life. A novice trainer will appreciate your advance thinking and be able to stand with confidence before the group. A more experienced trainer will use your plan as a road map with the journey's start and finish fixed, but the route flexible enough for side trips of spontaneity, student input and interaction.

In Step 6 you labelled each teaching point according to the type of learning (K = knowledge, A = attitude, and S = skill). On the chart below the most popular teaching techniques are matched to these three types of learning. The righthand columns indicate that all but the first two techniques have the potential for active learner participation.

Teaching technique	knowledge	attitude	skills	encourage participation
Lecture	◊			
Lecturette	◊	◊	◊	
Lecture-Forum	◊	◊		◊
Circle Response	◊	◊		◊
Spend-a-Penny				◊
Buzz Group	◊	◊		◊
Brainstorming	◊			◊
Guided Discussion		◊		◊
Role Play		◊	◊	◊
Reading/Research	◊	◊		◊
Field Trip/Project	◊	◊		◊
Learning Journal		◊	◊	◊
Demonstration/Practice		◊	◊	◊

There isn't enough space in *QUIP* to describe these teaching techniques in detail, but my INSTRUCTOR'S SURVIVAL KIT contains scores of step-by-step suggestions on when and how to use them. For now, I offer a synopsis to assist you in choosing.

MAY I SUGGEST...

LECTURE

The lecture works best when you want to impart facts, figures and information; when the material is needed for short-term retention; and when it is used as a preamble to a practical application. The lecture has limited use when the material is very detailed; when you are dealing with emotions, values, and attitudes; when your audience has little experience with formal education; and when the learners must apply the information in some practical way.

The basic rules for successful lecturing are:
- do not present more than six major points
- limit the presentation to 30 minutes
- present summaries at the start and finish
- pause frequently
- use visuals to support your points
- remember that the lecture is one-way communication
- let the audience know how questions will be handled.

LECTURETTE

The lecturette is a short lecture limited to about 10 minutes. By dividing a complex lecture into several lecturettes, you can deal more effectively with questions; you can ensure that your audience keeps up with the topic; and you can change the passive behavior of an audience with relevant activities between lecturettes.

LECTURE-FORUM

The lecture-forum blends a straight lecture with short reflection and question periods. It prompts the learner to review the points made, ask questions and relate all this to other materials. The trainer can prime the thinking pump. Instead of a 'closed' query "Are there any questions?", which may result in silence, the question becomes more 'open' when posed as, "How do you relate these two points to your work situation?"

CIRCLE RESPONSE

Circle response is a small group activity which gives all participants an opportunity to contribute and to be heard. After the trainer states the issue or question to be addressed, each person takes a turn to briefly state her or his ideas, opinions and feelings. No interruptions are allowed. Each speaker is limited to 10 to 30 seconds and the trainer may summarize the responses verbally or on the board.

SPEND-A-PENNY

This technique offers a quick way to generate group participation and deals with the dilemma of some people doing all the talking. Each participant is given three tokens (pennies, poker chips) and is instructed to spend them "as you like, when you feel like buying some uninterrupted air time". When learners have equal currency, they tend to use their "power" more carefully.

BUZZ GROUPS

These are small groups of three to five people, formed on the spot and dismantled immediately after the task is completed. They are used at any stage of a lecture or session to turn one-way into two-way communication. An example: after a brief presentation of theory, ask members to turn to their neighbors and form groups of 3 to 5 people. State a problem or issue and instruct the groups to deal with it in a specified time period, usually no more than 5 minutes. At the end of that time, ask for comments from the groups by way of a spokesperson from each or, if your class is large, from selected representatives.

BRAINSTORMING

Brainstorming has already been described in Step 1. It works well with small groups. Use it at the outset of a topic (to determine what people know or don't know); in the midst of a presentation (to deal with the content); or at the conclusion (to explore applications of the materials and to elicit questions and solutions).

GUIDED DISCUSSION

Potentially a free-for-all, a discussion can be carefully controlled. It can generate interesting comments and a sense of ownership by those who participate. The topic must be clear and the seating conducive to interacting. The trainer draws out quiet members and utilizes the energy of the more outspoken ones. When the discussion goes off topic, he brings it back; when members get into personal arguments, he focuses on the issue under discussion. A class discussion can be inserted at strategic points. It is useful at the outset of a new topic to find out what members' views are, after a lecture to help digest new information, or after an instructional event to deal with new questions and possible applications.

ROLE PLAYING

Role playing is best used when learners benefit from trying out new behavior in a controlled setting. Don't use it just to "have fun" or to "see how well you can act". There are four distinct phases in a well-run role play.

1. Set the scene by explaining what you propose to do. Ask for the group's cooperation and relate the role play to what has gone before or what will follow.
2. Assign specific roles and tasks to group members and ask the rest to observe and keep notes. Stick to time limits. Start and stop the action to keep on topic and to ensure that the role play brings out the issues you intended.
3. De-brief the roleplay. Ask the players to step out of role to report their experience. Observers share their insights and the trainer adds clarifications.
4. Finally, initiate a closure and generalization phase by posing the question "what have you learned ... how does it apply to your world?" The learners can begin to relate the roleplay to the larger picture.

OVER TO YOU...

Now work on your course.

Are your planning charts in clear view? Do you see the three columns headed "teaching techniques"? Then you are set to decide how the trainer and learner will interact.

Proceed along these lines:

☐ Concentrate on one objective at a time. For each teaching point, select the most appropriate teaching technique.

☐ Write the technique (and brief comments) on a sticker and place it next to the intended teaching point. For now, stick it in the middle column. Do this for all your objectives.

☐ As you decide which technique to assign, be guided by the matching table and the brief descriptions. Be generous: add your own ideas and techniques.

☐ When you have completed the first round of selection, pause and reflect. Are you satisfied with the way this course is unfolding?

☐ Ask yourself: "Who will be doing all the work?", or put another way, "Does my choice of teaching technique make for a teacher-centered or a learner-centered course?"

Teaching techniques can be placed on a continuum. At one end the trainer controls the process and at the other the learner. I believe that the trainer is primarily responsible for creating a stimulating environment and for presenting information in ways that let learners take charge of their own learning. For what kind of an atmosphere are you aiming? I suggest that you prescribe techniques with high trainer control at the start and then shift gradually to the learners assuming most of the control at the end.

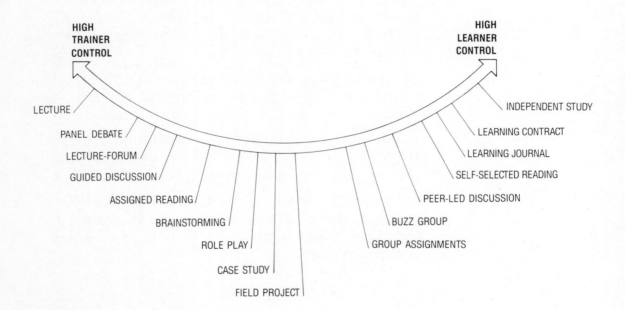

HIGH
TRAINER
CONTROL

HIGH
LEARNER
CONTROL

LECTURE

PANEL DEBATE

LECTURE-FORUM

GUIDED DISCUSSION

ASSIGNED READING

BRAINSTORMING

ROLE PLAY

CASE STUDY

FIELD PROJECT

INDEPENDENT STUDY

LEARNING CONTRACT

LEARNING JOURNAL

SELF-SELECTED READING

PEER-LED DISCUSSION

BUZZ GROUP

GROUP ASSIGNMENTS

Further refinements:

☐ Re-assess your choice of techniques in light of the diagram.

☐ Further refine the specifications by completing the lefthand and righthand columns (under "teaching techniques"). Add stickers to indicate the connecting pieces between teaching points: at the *beginning* of a teaching point, build in introductory remarks that set the scene and provide a link to the previous point(s). Toward the *end,* plan for summarizing, tying up of loose ends and bridging to the next teaching point(s).

☐ Now leave your charts alone for a while and get some distance from them. Let others have a peek.

☐ Ask an experienced trainer (or two) to look things over and give you the benefit of their experience.

☐ Dig out the participant profile (Worksheet 3) and assess how well your course plan might fit their expectations.

STOP

You are on the home stretch. You deserve a break and a reward for all the hard work. Treat yourself!

EXAMPLE

This is a partially completed planning chart.

COURSE: "THE COMPLETE BUTLER" **PLANNER:** BERTRAM WOOSTER

COMMENTS: DO THIS EARLY IN THE DAY

TOPIC	TEACHING POINTS	TEACHING TECHNIQUES		
		at the beginning	in the middle	towards the end
BREAKFAST SERVICE	**A** Proper tea is well worth the wait. There is only **one** way to make good tea. **A+K**	**LECTURETTE:** TRADITIONS OF TEA MAKING **SURVEY CLASS:** WHAT IS "A GOOD CUP OF TEA?"	EXPLAIN THE OBJECTIVES & HOW SESSION IS STRUCTURED.	
OBJECTIVE ... ABLE TO PREPARE A CORRECTLY BREWED POT OF TEA	Different varieties of tea blends produce different flavours: e.g. Earl Grey, Darjeeling, Irish Breakfast, English Breakfast, Prince of Wales. **K**		**LECTURETTE:** TEA VARIETIES (GO THROUGH HAND-OUT)	
	Three factors influence taste and quality of final products: 1. Water temperature. 2. Ratio of tea leaves to water. 3. Brewing time. **K**		**SURVEY CLASS:** "WHICH FACTORS INFLUENCE TASTE & QUALITY?" WRITE ON FLIPCHART.	
	A "A watched pot never boils." How to warm the pot prior to brewing. **S**		**DEMONSTRATE:** ("HOLD YOUR QUESTIONS 'TIL END OF MY DEMO")	
	The correct placement of tea bag or tea ball. How to boil water and pour over leaves. **A+S**		DEMO	**REPRESENTATION PRACTICE:** ASK 2 STUDENTS TO REPEAT DEMO
	How to maintain proper temperature of brewed tea. **S**		DEMO	• ANSWER QUESTIONS • NEXT SESSION ON "COFFEE"

NOTES

eight

Instruction stops when the student has learned, not when the bell rings.

--Robert Mager

Almost all really new ideas have a certain aspect of foolishness when they are first produced.

--A.N. Whitehead

BUILDING IN EVALUATION

*A*lmost there! You have this course planning routine well under control. Fat consulting contracts are coming your way. The Tahiti Horticultural Society and the Mikonos Chamber of Commerce are constantly on the phone, begging you to fly down to revamp their entire training program. There, it rings again. You reach for it and s l o w l y , your old office comes into focus. Rats! Still not done with *QUIP*. How many more Steps are there???

Hold on to your grounding cord; only three more to go. In the previous Steps (in case your dreams caused a lapse of memory) you have prescribed the *where*, the *what* and the *how*. Just ahead lies the task of measuring *how well* this has occurred.

The evaluation concentrates on the core elements of the course: *process* and *content*. By evaluating the process, you answer, "How do the learners view the course? What feedback can they give the trainer (and the designer)?" By evaluating the content, you find out "What has been learned and how far have the learners progressed toward mastery of the objectives?"

Before proceeding, decide which type of evaluation is needed. Some sort of process evaluation is a must for any course, especially a new one. You need to know how well your design worked under fire. The trainer and sponsor also have an interest in that information. Most of all, the learners are entitled to be heard from. Their feedback is valuable information.

I'll explain the process evaluation first and the content measures later. Suggestions for adding them to your planning charts are at the end of the chapter.

If you want to know what participants think of the trainer's efforts and also solicit their suggestions for improvements, use a simple evaluation form. Of the many in circulation, one consistently does a fine job for me. It touches all aspects of the course and leaves the door open for critical comments and suggestions for improvement.

DAILY QUESTIONNAIRE

1. What do you consider to have been today's most valuable experience?

   Why?

2. What aspect of today's program could have been strengthened?

   How?

3. Any additional comments?

   Your name _____
   optional

There is not enough space in *QUIP* to include more samples of evaluation forms. Several are included in my INSTRUCTOR'S SURVIVAL KIT and you are welcome to adapt them to your style or the occasion. Below are two resources: guidelines for the use of evaluation forms and a non-traditional procedure I call "speedy memo".

MAY I SUGGEST...

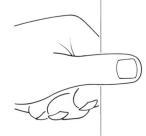

DO'S AND DO NOT'S OF PROCESS EVALUATION

♦ Do allow time in class for the completion of the form. Do it while the memories are still fresh.

♦ Don't let participants take the form home. The returns will be minimal.

♦ Do try to process the responses right away, while everyone is still there. This won't take long and learners can see the immediate impact of their input.

♦ Do on-the-spot evaluations throughout the course. It's easier to deal with feedback in small chunks. Avoid the dumping of penned-up feedback at the end when it's too late. Early on some changes can be made in mid-stream, others cannot. At least you will have had a chance to say so.

♦ Do feed the comments back to the group. For, instance, if you've collected evaluations at the end of Day II of a four-day workshop, start off the next day with a snappy summary of the comments. Then let them know what, if any, changes are planned. Such a matter-of-fact response fosters a cooperative spirit.

♦ Do keep track of evaluation comments after the course. They are valuable information when you plan the next event. It also assists the trainer and planner to assess their skills.

SPEEDY MEMO

Is a process evaluation with a difference. Easily interspersed with other activities, it requires no handouts, gets everyone involved, needs little discussion, and tends to be enjoyed -- because it's unusual. To make it work, the trainer ....

♦ halts the proceedings with, "I'd like us to take a moment to reflect on how we are doing. I'd like your honest opinion";

♦ describes the feedback desired, "how is the pace?", "what do you think of the session so far?", "how do you feel about the incident in the roleplay earlier?" (Just one question at a time);

♦ invites the startled, but certainly attentive group to "take a small piece of paper, half a sheet or less, any scrap will do and write just one word, an adjective, a noun, a verb that describes their answer to the question";

♦ quickly collects the bits of paper, mixes them up and asks a learner to read the replies out loud in rapid succession, without comments;

♦ responds to the comments.

The whole procedure should take no longer than 3 minutes. This works best with groups up to 20 participants. If yours is larger, ask people to form groups of five and to pass their comments to a spokesperson who reads out the comments. This still only takes about 10 minutes.

Content evaluation is typically needed when students have to jump a hurdle such as a course grade, final examination or a passing score. As well, the course sponsor may require "final marks" or a "pass/fail" determination.

Look at one of your objectives on a planning chart. Since you've specified the learning *outcome*, it won't be hard to figure out *what* to measure. *How* to measure is another cup of tea.

Here's a quick example from the course I mentioned earlier on "how to manage meetings". The objective:

The learner will be able to describe the difference between a "content" and a "process" intervention.

How would *you* measure someone's know-how? Please jot down your answer now. (Do it on separate paper to avoid marking your book).

_____

_____

_____

Likely you'd be asking the learner to define the types of interventions and then to differentiate between them. You could do this through a pencil-and-paper test or through verbal questioning.

Content evaluation can be achieved by a traditional written test or a creatively integrated activity. May I suggest a different approach (see "fishbowl" below)? It may take more time, but will cause fewer attacks of test anxiety and will provide the trainer with some unexpected "teachable moments". The choice is up to the designer-trainer team.

FISHBOWL

This describes a non-traditional way of evaluating content. The example is still "how to manage meetings"; the aim is to evaluate the learners' ability to describe the difference between content and process interventions.

Learners arrange their chairs in a fishbowl arrangement, with an inner and outer circle.

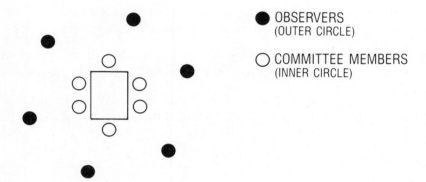

● OBSERVERS
(OUTER CIRCLE)

○ COMMITTEE MEMBERS
(INNER CIRCLE)

Learners seated in the middle (including a designated chairperson and various committee members) are given a topic to discuss in a simulated meeting. Their topic could be: How can we improve telephone manners throughout the organization? Those seated in the outer circle are assigned an observer role. They watch and record, using the "observation sheet" to tally the interactions and record a typical example for each type.

After sufficient time has gone by, stop the proceedings and ask the observers to share their comments.

OBSERVATION SHEET		
	Leader	Group Members
# of times I observed process interventions: One typical example is: _____ _____	///	//
# of times I observed content interventions: One typical example is: _____ _____	## /	/

Assign one observer per problem solver, or ask observers to report on the behavior of the leader and the group.

As well, each problem solver is asked to think back on the meeting and to use the Observation Sheet to rate his/her own intervention behavior.

After the observer reports, it is the trainer's job to draw out of the group the definitions and differences between content and process interventions; to question individuals to determine their confidence in the objective; to clarify misunderstandings; to challenge the group to think beyond the brief experiment; and to apply what has been learned to other meeting situations.

MAY I SUGGEST...

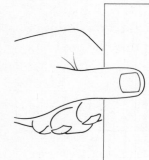

TYPES OF TESTS

Written tests that measure the desired learning outcome can be divided into two groups:

Supply type tests, where the trainee supplies the answer by:
- essay
- filling blanks to complete statements
- short-answer replies to questions.

Selection type tests, where the trainee selects the answer by:

- determining whether statements are true or false
- matching questions to a choice of answers
- multiple-choice.

For practical advice on developing tests, see:

Norman Gronlund, CONSTRUCTING ACHIEVEMENT TESTS (3rd ed.) Englewood Cliffs, NJ: Prentice-Hall, 1982.
HOW TO CONSTRUCT ACHIEVEMENT TESTS Englewood Cliffs, NJ: Prentice Hall, 1988.
Robert Mager, MEASURING INSTRUCTIONAL RESULTS (2nd ed.) Belmont, CA: D.S. Lake Publ., 1984.

OVER TO YOU...

Now work on your evaluation strategy.

Place a sticker in the box under the heading "evaluation" on each planning chart. For *content* evaluation, show which teaching points are to be covered and by what type of procedure. For *process* evaluation, indicate the form or process you recommend to the trainer.

With the completion of Step 8 the key pieces of your course puzzle are now in place. Before you call room service to put the Champagne on ice however, take a step back to reflect on your handiwork.

☐ Is this a good time to connect with your cooperators who assisted you early on? Why not invite a select few to preview your charts? Walk them through the completed Steps, explain your strategy and listen to their comments and questions. I bet they'll be impressed by your attention to detail and the sheer volume of work.

☐ This is also a good time to look for "?"-marked and "parked" stickers. Tidy up. Do you need to keep them any longer? Seek any missing information so that you can decide with confidence.

☐ Make a "to do" list of any odds and ends that come to mind as you look over your charts.

This is a partially completed planning chart.

COURSE: "THE COMPLETE BUTLER" **PLANNER:** BERTRAM WOOSTER

COMMENTS: DO THIS EARLY IN THE DAY

TOPIC / OBJECTIVE	TEACHING POINTS	TEACHING TECHNIQUES		
		at the beginning	in the middle	towards the end
TOPIC BREAKFAST SERVICE	**A** Proper tea is well worth the wait. There is only **one** way to make good tea. **A+K**	**LECTURETTE:** TRADITIONS OF TEA MAKING **SURVEY CLASS:** WHAT IS "A GOOD CUP OF TEA?"	EXPLAIN THE OBJECTIVES & HOW SESSION IS STRUCTURED.	
OBJECTIVE . . . ABLE TO PREPARE A CORRECTLY BREWED POT OF TEA	Different varieties of tea blends produce different flavours: e.g. Earl Grey, Darjeeling, Irish Breakfast, English Breakfast, Prince of Wales. **K**		**LECTURETTE:** TEA VARIETIES (GO THROUGH HAND-OUT)	
	Three factors influence taste and quality of final products: 1. Water temperature. 2. Ratio of tea leaves to water. 3. Brewing time. **K**		**SURVEY CLASS:** "WHICH FACTORS INFLUENCE TASTE & QUALITY?" WRITE ON FLIPCHART.	
	A "A watched pot never boils." How to warm the pot prior to brewing. **S**		**DEMONSTRATE:** ("HOLD YOUR QUESTIONS 'TIL END OF MY DEMO")	
	The correct placement of tea bag or tea ball. How to boil water and pour over leaves. **A+S**		DEMO	**REPRESENTATION PRACTICE:** ASK 2 STUDENTS TO REPEAT DEMO
	How to maintain proper temperature of brewed tea. **S**		DEMO	• ANSWER QUESTIONS • NEXT SESSION ON "COFFEE"
		"ASK 2 DIFFERENT STUDENTS TO SUMMARIZE LESSON."	• MULTIPLE CHOICE QUIZ (AS PART OF END-OF-DAY EXAM	GROUP COMMENTS ON 2-STUDENT DEMO IN LIGHT OF SUMMARY.

EVALUATION

RESOURCES

Assessment, evaluation

Angelo, T. A., & Cross, K. P. (1993). *Classroom assessment techniques: a handbook for college teachers.* (2nd ed.). San Francisco: Jossey-Bass.

Fenwick, T., & Parson, M. J. (1999). *The art of evaluation: a handbook for educators and trainers.* Thompson Educational Publ.

MacGregor, J. (Ed.). (1993). *Student self-evaluation: fostering reflective learning.* New Directions for Teaching and Learning, No. 56. San Francisco: Jossey-Bass.

Moran, J. A. (1997). *Assessing adult learning: a guide for practitioners.* Malabar, FL: Krieger Publishing.

Speck, B. W. (2000). *Grading students' classroom writing: issues and strategies.* San Francisco: Jossey-Bass.

Vella, J., Berardinelli, P., & Burrow, J. (1997). *How do they know they know? Evaluating adult learning.* San Francisco: Jossey-Bass.

Walvoord, B. E., & Anderson, V. J. (1998). *Effective grading: a tool for learning and assessment.* San Francisco: Jossey-Bass.

Professional development for teachers

Brookfield, S. D. (1995). *Becoming a critically reflective teacher.* San Francisco: Jossey-Bass.

Centra, J. A. (1993). *Reflective faculty evaluation.* San Francisco: Jossey-Bass.

Clift, R. T., & others (1990). *Encouraging reflective practice in education.* New York: Teachers College Press.

Cranton, P. (1996). *Professional development as transformative learning: new perspectives for teachers of adults.* San Francisco: Jossey-Bass.

Cranton, P. (2001). *Becoming an authentic teacher in higher education.* Malabar, FL: Krieger Publishing.

Lawler, P. A., & King, K. P. (2001). *Planning for effective faculty development: using adult learning strategies.* Malabar, FL: Krieger Publishing.

Moran, J. J. (2001). *Collaborative professional development for teachers of adults.* Malabar, FL: Krieger Publishing.

Tremmerl, R. (1993). Zen and the art of reflective practice in teacher education. *Harvard Educational Review, 63,* 4, 434-458. Available: www.edreview.org/harvard93/wi93/w93trem.htm

nine

Give us the tools and we will do the work.

--Winston Churchill

Begin at the beginning and go on till you come to the end; then stop.

--The King, in ''Alice in Wonderland''

DESIGNATING RESOURCES

*T*his is *it*. Definitely the last Step! Put the Champagne on ice. Another hour or so and you will have completed the planning process. What remains are three housekeeping chores. You still have to:

♦ determine the resources the trainer will need:

By *resources* I mean the various items the trainer has to organize prior to the course, including: training facilities, furniture arrangements, printed handouts, audio-visual equipment and special demonstration and practice materials.

♦ estimate the time each objective requires:

A *time estimate* is needed to count the minutes it should take to cover the objectives and teaching points. If the overall course length is pre-determined, your planned activities must neatly fill the time.

♦ write the lesson plan so that the trainer can take over:

A *lesson plan* is a chronological description of how you envisage the course will unfold. It provides the stage directions for the trainer and learners -- from the starting "Welcome to this course" to the parting "Good night".

MAY I SUGGEST...

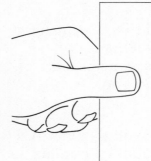

RESOURCES

There is one way of accomplishing this without much pain but with a high chance of catching all the essential details.

☐ Take one chart at a time and re-acquaint yourself with the information posted under the headings "teaching techniques" and "evaluation procedures".

☐ Determine the resources needed for the prescribed activities. For instance, if the trainer must demonstrate the use of a piece of equipment, then say so and post your directions in the "resources" column. Do the same for furniture arrangements, printed handouts and audio-visual equipment.

☐ The "remarks" column is a place where you can leave little messages to the trainer: "Check the video before the group arrives", "Remind them to read and analyze the case prior to class", "Hold handouts until after the lecture".

CALCULATING COURSE TIME

At your first try, the "time available" and "time needed" rarely match. You may have to go back to each chart and either shorten or lengthen the time. To save time, you may have to limit the number of teaching points, reduce the time for the completion of an objective, or remove an objective altogether. To stretch the time, you have the options of expanding certain time allowances or of adding one or two objectives to fill the time frame.

Protect the integrity of your design and consult with your cooperators during this shuffling process. Consult with your trainer or subject expert whenever you wish to increase or decrease content. Look back to the early Steps for content items that can be added or deleted.

☐ Now estimate the time it will take to complete each objective. Make allowances for the introductory, middle and closing activities posted next to the teaching points. Post the total time estimate in the chart's bottom left-hand corner.

☐ Add up the total time for the entire course. Allow for administrative functions (such as attendance, collection of registration slips), ice-breaking activities and refreshment and meal breaks along the way.

After some back and forth arranging, a rough outline for a day-long workshop could look like this:

```
                                  Start 9 am
Registration check            10    min
Introductions                 10
Go over course outline        10
Objective 1                   40
Morning break 10:10 am        15
Objective 2                   60
Film                          15
Objective 3                   20 _____ 180 mins./3 hrs.

Lunch at noon
                              Reconvene at 1 pm
Any questions?                 5
Brief evaluation               5
Objective 4                   40
Case Study (Obj. 3&4)         30
Objective 5                   40
Break 3 pm                    15
Task groups (Obj. 3,4,5)      60
Discussion                    25
Question & Answers            15
Course Evaluation              5 _____ 240 mins./4 hrs.
End by 5:00 pm
```

After further refinements the plan can be re-written to show real times and a brief content description. The following is from a two-day "training techniques" course and was given to the participants when they arrived:

Course: Basic Training Skills
OVERVIEW
Day I

9:00	Introductions
9:10	Course goals and objectives
9:20	Expectations: What would success look like?
9:40	Get-acquainted exercise
9:50	Break
10:05	Mini-workshop: Writing learning objectives
10:55	Impromptu training practice
12:00	LUNCH
1:00	Improptu training - continued
1:40	Mini-workshop: Planning a training session
2:45	Break
3:00	Mini-workshop, continued
3:30	Mini-workshop: Using the flip chart
4:00	Individual planning for tomorrow
4:15	Day I evaluation; individual consultations
4:30	End of Day I

Day II

9:00	Unfinished business Summary of Day I evaluations
9:15	Practice sessions
10:30	Break
10:45	Practice sessions
12:00	LUNCH
1:00	Practice sessions
3:00	Break
3:15	Mini-workshop: Using the overhead projector
4:15	Course evaluation
4:30	End of course

MAY I SUGGEST...

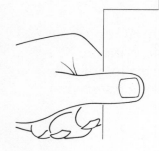

LESSON PLANS

Decide on a lesson plan format. Transfer your "stage directions" from the planning charts to the lesson plan. Give both to the trainer.

EXAMPLES

There are two ways to communicate your plan to the trainer. One is to arrange the plan in narrative form as shown in this excerpt from a course on "basic communication skills":

Time Activities

----

2 min   Ask learners to find a partner, someone they are reasonably comfortable with. They will share their experience from the previous 'guided fantasy'. Spread duos over the room to achieve some privacy.

12   Ask learners to read handbook page 14 one more time. Any questions?

        As they talk to each other about their fantasy, suggest they share only what they are comfortable with. They will have 10 minutes.

        Call time at 5 and 10 minutes.

5   Go over the checklist for 'good feedback' in the handbook, page 15. Ask each learner to write memo to their listening partner.

6   Ask the pairs to read the memo to each other. The recipient is "to just listen, don't defend or explain".

Another, more detailed layout shows pertinent directions on one page: time allowance, objective reference, description of trainer and learner activities, text reference, handout and overhead transparency reference.

MIN	OBJ	INSTRUCTOR'S ACTIVITIES	TEXT PAGE	LEARNER'S ACTIVITIES	INSTRUCTIONAL AIDS
10	3.1	Introduce topic of reservations. Ask why they are necessary - and what would happen if there was no such thing. Develop list on board or flipchart. Ask if anyone had experience with making a reservation at a hotel: good or bad experience?		Contribute ideas.	Flipchart, feltpen. Chalkboard, chalk.
5		Describe functions a reservation system must be able to handle, regardless of the type of operation, clientele and volume.	p. 81		
10		Explain the routes by which potential guest can reach an operation to make reservation. Explain role of various "agents", the cost and benefits to the hotel.	p. 82		OT #3
20	3.2	Using actual forms for each pair of students, lead them through the filling out of a basic reservation form. Different forms are used, but the basic reason for basic information remains.	p. 86-88	Working in two's will fill out res. forms from information provided by their partner.	OT #4
		Explain terminology and abbreviations used: GTD, 6 pm, VIP, special rate, etc.			
	3.3	Explain differences in handling individual & group bookings. Who should handle it?	p. 102		OT #5
10	3.1	Explain how/why reservations are charted and how this will differ in approach from one op. to another. The following charting exercise will give students a chance to learn the skills involved.	p. 93 - -		OT #6 OT #7 , 7a
60		Charting exercise: instructions in package.			
		Be available for consultation; it is not necessary that everyone finishes it, but that s/he has a good understanding how/why this is done and must be done with precision/care.		Following instructions and working through the exercise.	HO: Reservations Charting Exercise

OT = overhead transparency
HO = printed handout

Now the planning chart is complete.

COURSE: "THE COMPLETE BUTLER"   **PLANNER:** BERTRAM WOOSTER

COMMENTS: DO THIS EARLY IN THE DAY

TOPIC	TEACHING POINTS	TEACHING TECHNIQUES		
		at the beginning	in the middle	towards the end
BREAKFAST SERVICE	**A** Proper tea is well worth the wait. There is only **one** way to make good tea. **A+K**	**LECTURETTE:** TRADITIONS OF TEA MAKING. **SURVEY CLASS:** WHAT IS "A GOOD CUP OF TEA?"	EXPLAIN THE OBJECTIVES & HOW SESSION IS STRUCTURED.	
OBJECTIVE ... ABLE TO PREPARE A CORRECTLY BREWED POT OF TEA	Different varieties of tea blends produce different flavours. e.g. Earl Grey, Darjeeling, Irish Breakfast, English Breakfast, Prince of Wales. **K**		**LECTURETTE:** TEA VARIETIES (GO THROUGH HAND-OUT)	
	Three factors influence taste and quality of final products: 1. Water temperature. 2. Ratio of tea leaves to water. 3. Brewing time. **K**		**SURVEY CLASS:** "WHICH FACTORS INFLUENCE TASTE & QUALITY?" WRITE ON FLIPCHART.	
	A "A watched pot never boils." How to warm the pot prior to brewing. **S**		**DEMONSTRATE:** ("HOLD YOUR QUESTIONS 'TIL END OF MY DEMO")	
	The correct placement of tea bag or tea ball. How to boil water and pour over leaves. **A+S**		DEMO	**REPRESENTATION PRACTICE:** ASK 2 STUDENTS TO REPEAT DEMO
	How to maintain proper temperature of brewed tea. **S**		DEMO	• ANSWER QUESTIONS • NEXT SESSION ON "COFFEE"
		"ASK 2 DIFFERENT STUDENTS TO SUMMARIZE LESSON"	• MULTIPLE CHOICE QUIZ (AS PART OF END-OF-DAY EXAM)	GROUP COMMENTS ON 2-STUDENT DEMO IN LIGHT OF SUMMARY.
TIME		• FLIPCHART, PAPER, EASEL, PENS • ALL TEA MAKING PARAPENALIA FOR TRAINER & STUDENTS.	**HANDOUT:** "TEA VARIETIES"	ARRANGE DEMO TABLE AND FLIPCHART SO ALL CAN SEE & HEAR.
30 MINUTES MAXIMUM	ASK GROUP TO STAND DURING THE ENTIRE SESSION. "BUTLERS NEED STRONG LEGS."	START TO BOIL WATER DURING INTO LECTURE.	**EMPHASIZE:** • SAFETY • SANITATION • SPEED	**OPTIONAL:** TASTE EACH CUP OF TEA.

(right margin labels: EVALUATION, RESOURCES, REMARKS)

NOTES

ten

We shall not cease from exploration
And in the end of all our exploring
Will be to arrive where we started
And know the place for the first time.

--T.S. Eliot

Try, there is no try.
There is only do or not do.

--Yoda in ''The Empire Strikes Back''

REVISING YOUR PLAN

FROM THE DIARY OF A LONE PLANNER

*Peter has invited me to
close his book.*

I feel like I am addressing the graduating class and I
want to leave you with something you've probably
figured out already. Yes, the planning process never
really ends. Like the man who "will ride forever 'neath
the streets of Boston", your project will live on and on.

Back in 1984 when I was a novice, I was asked to
design my first course. It was to be used by trainers
who had a wide range of skills - - somewhere between
a beautician and a rocket scientist. I didn't understand
the diversity that I was going to meet, but I was young
and eager to please the boss.

I armed myself with weighty texts on instructional
planning. I poured through reams of comments and
suggestions by "representative" learners whom the
course was supposed to satisfy. I borrowed some
designs that were "like" what I wanted - - but in the
end, nothing seemed to fit. I was looking for easy
answers.

Naively, I was convinced that if I could just take the
same old information and say it in a different way I'd
be away to the races. My boss, always with one eye on
the budget, agreed. "Say the same thing, just say it
better," he said.

To complicate matters, my subject was customer service
-- specifically, ensuring that government telephone
operators' attitudes were up to scratch. Why couldn't I
be the one who got to design pencil sharpening? I
blindly stepped into the pool of attitude objectives.

In a panic, I went to a two-day seminar on design. The class was split into pairs. My partner was a Fire Chief who needed to write a design that taught rookies how to climb a ladder. He ended up with one objective and two teaching points! This was looking harder all the time.

After two months, the design was "complete" (ha!) with the preliminary manuals and participant books printed. I chose a small town to pilot the material.

The course was to be held in the local high school. It was spring break and the janitor had just waxed the floors. "By the way," he said as he disappeared into the bowels of the school, "no body (sic) wears the shoes on *my* floor!" Panty hose on a waxed floor has the same effect as climbing a greased pole. What does a good trainer do? Improvise!

I took out my slippers with pig's heads from my traveling bag. This did get the attention of my would-be trainees but not in the way I had intended.

It got worse. During the design stage, while planning a communications exercise, (much like "fishbowl"), I had innovatively come up with a modification. Why hadn't the experts thought of this? I purposely eliminated the task of observer from the exercise. This would give everyone the chance to role play. It also did away with the need for observation sheets to keep a record of the interactions. Brilliant, right? (I could have used some expert cooperators about then).

Back to reality. After the actual role play had taken place and I gave the instructions for the feedback stage, it finally dawned on me that I had been the only observer! While I was dealing with one pair, 17 other pairs broke out into an assortment of confusions and arguments. To say that the Mayor had to declare "martial law" is a bit of an overstatement; besides, he didn't have the time. *He* was bitterly disputing the feedback of another trainee! To compound my mistake, I had neglected to write up instructions for the role play. Complete disaster.

The point is that I really wasn't prepared -- I could have used the Instructional Planner *and* the Survival Kit! I learned that the design process doesn't end until you have practised it enough times to debug it.

Well, you've just read this book. My advice to you at this stage of your planning is to keep your sense of humor; remember "the best laid schemes of mice and men" and Murphy's Law, and most importantly, never be satisfied with the final product. The minute it's down on paper, it's subject to re-write!

Good luck!

Dawn M. Saintsbury

ERIC Digests

Funded by the U.S. Department of Education, these Digests capture recent developments on selected topics. Digests are available on-line and may be down-loaded and duplicated. The following is a sampling of interesting topics; for the full articles, go to the web address given next to each title. For your own search, go to http://ericir.syr.edu/Eric/. The following abstracts are taken from the ERIC website.

Inclusive Adult Learning Environments. ERIC Digest No. 162. Available: www.ed.gov/databases/ERIC_Digests/ed385779.html

Ever since Malcolm Knowles introduced the concept of learning climate, adult educators have been aware of how the environment affects learning. As reflected in the words of the returning woman student quoted here, however, adults may still find some learning environments to be inhospitable. Rather than learners trying to change who they are so that they will "fit in," adult educators must create learning environments in which all learners can thrive. Following an overview of changing conceptions of adult learning environments, this Digest describes what it means to create an inclusive learning environment, examines some related issues, and presents some guidelines for structuring inclusive learning environments.

Teaching Adults: Is It Different? ERIC Digest No. 82. Available: www.ed.gov/databases/ERIC_Digests/ed305495.html

The adult education literature generally supports the idea that teaching adults should be approached in a different way than teaching children and adolescents, groups sometimes referred to as preadults. The assumption that teachers of adults should use a style of teaching different from that used with preadults is based on "informed professional opinion; philosophical assumptions associated with humanistic psychology and progressive education; and a growing body of research and theory on adult learning, development, and socialization." Following a discussion of the major model underlying this assumption, this Digest examines research that investigates differences in these teaching styles and suggests considerations for practice.

Guidelines for Working with Adult Learners. ERIC Digest No. 154. Available: www.ed.gov/databases/ERIC_Digests/ed377313.html

"Adults vote with their feet," a favorite adage of adult educators, is frequently used to describe a characteristic of adult learners. In most circumstances, adults are not captive learners and, if the learning situation does not suit their needs and interests, they will simply stop coming. In discussing adult education, Knowles distinguished between teacher-centered and learner-centered instruction. He promoted the latter because it viewed learners as mutual partners in the learning endeavor. Known as the andragogical model, the use of learner-centered instruction—which supports addressing the needs and interests of learners—is regularly championed in the literature as the most effective way to teach adults. However, Merriam & Caffarella assert that "adult learning in formal settings, for the most part, is still instructor designed and directed." Given the wide support for learner involvement, the discrepancy between adult education theory and practice is perplexing. How can instructors of adults become more learner centered in their practice? This Digest suggests guidelines and strategies that can be used in formal settings by instructors of adults to involve learners more effectively.

Teaching Adults with Learning Disabilities. ERIC Digest No. 99. Available: www.ed.gov/databases/ERIC_Digests/ed321156.html

Adult educators concur that youngsters with learning disabilities (LD) do not simply outgrow them. They become adults with LD, and many of them participate in adult education programs. This Digest discusses the number of adult learners with LD, identifies relevant issues, describes intervention strategies, and suggests specific techniques that adult educators can use with their LD students.

Adult learner retention revisited. ERIC Digest No. 166 by Sandra Kerka. Available: www.ericacve.org/docgen.asp?tbl=digests&ID=19

Adult learner retention continues to hold the attention of adult educators in every type of program. Although the reasons students leave and the strategies for keeping them may differ from adult basic education (ABE) to higher education, the goal of retention is the same: to keep learners in programs until they achieve their goals. In any program, adults are largely voluntary participants, but the student role is just one of many roles and responsibilities competing for their time and attention. In fact, personal reasons such as family problems, lack of child care, and job demands are often cited as the cause of withdrawal. At the same time, adults usually have pragmatic, focused reasons for participating and will leave whenever they feel their goals have been met or if they feel the program will not satisfy their goals. Personal/job factors may seem to be beyond institutional control, whereas program satisfaction is something educators can improve. This Digest provides an updated look at research on retention in adult education and suggests effective practices for different settings.

Situated learning in adult education. ERIC Digest No. 195 by David Stein. Available: www.ericacve.org/docgen.asp?tbl=digests&ID=48

In the situated learning approach, knowledge and skills are learned in the contexts that reflect how knowledge is obtained and applied in everyday situations. Situated cognition theory conceives of learning as a sociocultural phenomenon rather than the action of an individual acquiring general information from a decontextualized body of knowledge.This Digest presents an overview of the concepts related to applying situated cognition in adult learning. It should be noted that situated learning theory has not yet produced precise models or prescriptions for learning in classroom settings.

Transformative learning and the journey of individuation, ERIC Digest No. 223 by John M. Dirkx. Available: www.ericacve.org/docgen.asp?tbl=digests&ID=108

Over the last 20 years, transformation theory has deepened our understanding of what it means to learn in adulthood. Collectively, the work of Paulo Freire, Phyllis Cunningham, Laurent Daloz, and Jack Mezirow, among others, addresses the sociocultural and personal dimensions of transformative learning. Dominant views of transformative learning emphasize rational, cognitive processes related to critical reflection. An additional perspective on transformation, however, has emerged, led by Robert Boyd and his colleagues. This work focuses on deeper emotional and spiritual dimensions of learning that many have suggested are underdeveloped in dominant conceptions of transformative learning. This Digest summarizes and expands on Boyd's notion of transformative learning, discussing the role of image, symbol, ritual, fantasy, and imagination in transformation.

Web-based training. ERIC Digest No. 218 by Bettina Lankard Brown. Available: www.ericacve.org/docgen.asp?tbl=digests&ID=103

Education and training via the World Wide Web are growing rapidly. Reduced training costs, world-wide accessibility, and improved technological capabilities have made electronic instructional delivery to adult learners a viable alternative to classroom instruction. This Digest examines the efficacy of Web-based (WBT) training, including issues of market demand, learner participation, training options, and program design. It also discusses learning outcomes and gives suggestions for how these outcomes can be improved through implementation of appropriate instructional design principles.

APPENDIX

Worksheet 1: *IDENTIFYING TOPICS*

Course Title:

_____

Topics to be included:

1. _____
2. _____
3. _____
4. _____
5. _____
6. _____
7. _____
8. _____
9. _____
10. _____
11. _____
12. _____
13. _____
14. _____
15. _____

Worksheet 2: *LIST OF COOPERATORS*

Name	Why this person?
_____	_____
_____	_____
_____	_____
_____	_____
_____	_____
_____	_____
_____	_____
_____	_____
_____	_____

Summary notes of my discussions:

_____

_____

_____

_____

_____

_____

_____

_____

_____

_____

_____

_____

Worksheet 3: *PARTICIPANT PROFILE*

You can help us design a course on _____.
We want to make sure that we develop a course that meets the learning needs of people like you. Please complete this brief questionnaire with as much detail as you wish. It should take no more than 5 minutes of your time.

Your name (optional) _____

Your present job title or occupational function:

_____

_____

How many years have you held your present title or performed your occupational function: _____ years

Your gender: Female / Male

Your age group: Between 20 and 30
(check one)   between 30 and 40
                between 40 and 50
                between 50 and 60

Briefly list any course you have taken during the last three years that may be related to the one we are planning:

_____

_____

_____

_____

Which two words best describe your favorite instructor?:

_____

Which two words best describe the instructor you like least?:

_____

Worksheet 4: *MOST IMPORTANT TOPICS*

After consultation and reflection, write up your list of most important topics.

Course: _____

The most **important** topics are:

* _____

* _____

* _____

* _____

* _____

* _____

* _____

* _____

* _____

* _____

* _____

* _____

* _____

* _____

* _____

* _____

* _____

* _____

* _____

* _____

* _____

Worksheet 5: *COURSE TITLE*

Complete this worksheet in 4 stages.

1. Fill in the title you have been using in your preliminary planning. Put down also the one traditionally used in your setting.

   _____

   _____

2. Re-write the old title. Try for active verbs that convey the flavor of what you envisage.

   _____

   _____

3. Check it against each criterion below. Add your own as they occur to you. Take corrective action if you are unable to place a checkmark against an item.

The course title . . .

   ☐ conveys the content.
   ☐ gives a sense of the process.
   ☐ uses clearly understood words.
   ☐ fits into the list of other courses offered.
   ☐ meets the approval of the sponsor.
   ☐ _____

4. Show just the title to your cooperators. What do they *think* the course is about? Does their interpretation match your intention? Record their impressions, then revise (if necessary) or be satisfied (if the title conveyed your message fully).

Record of reactions

   _____

   _____

   _____

   _____

   _____

   _____

   _____

Reproduced with permission. "The (Quick) Instructional Planner" by Peter Renner.
All Rights Reserved. © Vancouver, B.C.: Training Associates, 1988.

Worksheet 6: *COURSE DESCRIPTION*

1. Write your description. Start off where your course title ends, enlarge upon it and anticipate the reader's questions.

    _____

    _____

    _____

    _____

    _____

    _____

    _____

    _____

    _____

    _____

2. Read the questions that follow and honestly evaluate your work.

    My course description . . .

    ☐ conveys the course content.
    ☐ gives a sense of the process.
    ☐ uses clearly understood words.
    ☐ indicates level of instruction and prerequisites.
    ☐ informs potential trainers.
    ☐ informs potential participants.
    ☐ meets the approval of the sponsor.
    ☐ fits the brochure / calendar in style and length.
    ☐ says exactly what I want it to say.
    ☐ _____

3. If you think that your description "fails" any of these, re-write until it "passes". Then be satisfied!

4. Show your shiny new title and course description to at least one cooperator. See your Worksheet #2 for the names of the people you consulted earlier. Record their reaction. Incorporate their ideas.

Worksheet 7: *PLANNING OBJECTIVES*

Course Title: _____

My planning objectives are:

* _____

_____

* _____

_____

* _____

_____

* _____

_____

* _____

_____

* _____

_____

* _____

_____

* _____

_____

* _____

_____

* _____

_____

* _____

_____

* _____

_____

Worksheet 8: *PROCESS OBJECTIVES*

Course Title: _____

My process objectives are:

*
_____

_____

*
_____

_____

*
_____

_____

*
_____

_____

*
_____

_____

*
_____

_____

*
_____

_____

*
_____

_____

*
_____

_____

*
_____

_____

*
_____

_____

*
_____

_____

Worksheet 9: *LEARNING OBJECTIVES*

Topic: _____

Course Title: _____

Objectives:

1. _____
   _____
   _____
   _____

2. _____
   _____
   _____
   _____

3. _____
   _____
   _____
   _____

4. _____
   _____
   _____
   _____

5. _____
   _____
   _____
   _____

A rule of thumb: If you have to write more than five objectives per topic, you are biting off more than is practical. Split the topic into two. The grouping of objectives becomes more manageable.